No Human Touch

Paul Halpin

New Wine Press

New Wine Press
PO Box 17
Chichester
West Sussex PO20 6YB
England

ISBN: 1 874367 54 X

Typeset by CRB Associates, Reepham, Norfolk.
Printed in England by Clays Ltd, St Ives plc.

Contents

No Human Touch

No human touch could have found its way
To that cold, cold heart,
That heart of stone, calloused through time.
Don't touch, don't touch,
The door is closed, permanently.
I've only known darkness:
Light has never been needed here.

Someone knocking, someone seeking, asking.
Someone in the blackness, in the coldness.
Why it's me! Knocking, asking and seeking.
Something unfamiliar touching my cold,
stony calloused heart.

Love has found a way in!
It really was me knocking, seeking, asking.
My heart begins to warm, then to melt.
Something touches that place.
Then like a warm breeze, someone whispers,
'Let me fill that space
With light, with "my" heart.
You now live, you now know life.'
But this is no human touch, my child,
But Jesus.
'I heard you knock,
I heard you ask,
And I saw you seek.
Here I am.'

Paul Halpin

Preface

When I first toyed with the idea of writing *No Human Touch*, the thought that I, an uneducated ex-addict, could accomplish such a task, brought back all the old feelings of total inadequacy that had dominated my whole life.

But I pressed on with a desire for once in my life to start and actually finish something. Having the manuscript published would be a bonus, but it was the starting and completion that really spurred me on.

I have tried to share in this book not only the hopelessness of alcohol and drug addiction but also to share the real hope and possibility that miracles can happen, that they can become a reality for those who perhaps society has written off as hopeless cases. On the streets of this world, we can witness for ourselves many thousands of our fellow humans addicted to alcohol and other substances. Alcohol- and drug-related criminal offences increase by the hour, thus swelling the confines of our penal institutions.

No Human Touch was never meant to be a

religious book, and neither is it, but rather a story of one man's search for an answer to what was a miserable existence and an escape from the bondage of chronic addiction. My personal experience was freedom through a very real experience with God and other humans who showed me love and compassion.

Many years of my life were spent in prisons and other institutions which I've written about in these pages that follow. But in its entirety, it's a story of a different sort of prison that only God could free me from. Thus it is indeed only by God's touch, not a human one, that I am alive and free today.

I hope and pray that in the simplicity in which I have written, God will use this true story to bring freedom to at least one other human being.

Foreword

There is nothing more fascinating about mankind than temperament. This uniqueness separates one person from another. It is a force that can destroy a normal person unless it is disciplined and directed. Therefore it is our temperament that provides our strengths and our weaknesses.

Paul Halpin's story is about trying to overcome a life full of abuse, addiction, crime and recidivism. He writes in graphic detail about his weaknesses and his daily battles to survive in a world where he doesn't fit in. Blinded by his pain and a refusal to conform, the darkness gets deeper. He wants to change but has no power to do so, flirting with the truth, yet never wanting to own it or wear it, as truth often demands change. Paul lives for many years in the 'now' mode, taking no responsibility for his own wrong decisions and choices, his life slowly ebbing away. Dramatically one day, he finally sees himself for what he is, and the light is switched on. Finally he gets serious with God and gets in touch with the only power that can bring about **lasting change**!

True freedom rests on individual responsibility, integrity, effort and courage but, most importantly, on personal salvation through Jesus Christ. Paul met the conditions and found that freedom. He has earned the right to share that testimony with others who find themselves on the long road to nowhere. It is a powerful testimony to the magnitude of God's love, patience and abundant grace!

Noel Fellowes
Christian Prison Ministries

Chapter 1

Into the Wilderness

My dad was an alcoholic. Alcohol eventually took his life. The death certificate would have said 'brain haemorrhage' but I know, and he knew, that alcohol destroyed him.

From an early age I was fascinated by alcohol. My father gave me glasses of stout which I discovered very early on in life lifted me both physically and mentally out of a world that I didn't want to be in. From the moment I experienced alcohol's dream-like effect on my person, I decided that this was how I always wanted to feel. I could understand now my father's preoccupation with the stuff that eventually took his life.

My school years, such as they were, ended in an approved school in Essex. I was given £7 and a train ticket to Hertfordshire where my mother and father lived, by now separately. I got as far as Liverpool Street station in London. As I sat myself down in the station bar, it seemed the most natural thing for me to do. I was just fifteen. I felt a stirring uneasiness in my stomach but then I remembered how the dark coloured stout had very quickly lifted

11

that uneasiness when my father had given me the stuff. 'It'll make a man a ye' he would say in his sing-along Irish brogue.

'Yes, young man, what'll it be?' said the middle-aged woman behind the bar.

'Err, um, a pint of Guinness luv, please' I replied in a voice which was meant to sound as though I'd been ordering pints at bars for years. I watched her pull the pint. Her eyes met mine just once, and I thought for one moment she would say something about my age; I didn't look eighteen at all. But no – she brought the drink to me, I paid her, and she gave me change. I lifted the pint glass to my lips and drank deeply, put the glass down and began to take in my surroundings – the various posters advertising different beers and spirits and also cigarettes. I had the makings of a cigarette in my jacket pocket. I rolled one, put it in my mouth and lit up. Here I was then, pint at the ready, ciggy in hand, ready to face what? I didn't know: I really didn't know. I'd spent most of my formative years in various institutions and at fifteen I was out in the real world.

I ordered another drink and included a whisky to chase it down with. I drank the whisky in one gulp and waited for the desired effect. It didn't make me feel sick as it thought I might. I followed it with a mouthful of stout. I looked directly in front of me at the bar and saw my own reflection – a very lonely boy of fifteen. I suddenly felt I never wanted to step outside that bar. I had no idea what lay ahead. I had already made up my mind I wasn't going to either of my parents. I didn't want to think any more. I ordered more drink. I so desperately wanted to talk to someone. There was a middle-aged man on the barstool next but one to me. He sat staring down into his large glass of spirits. I watched him for a while. He drank several more large drinks, as I did. He never had to ask for his glass to be filled: the barmaid seemed to have a built-in radar which homed in on his glass whenever he emptied it. I felt quite envious of this unspoken relationship that they had.

I found him looking at me, then my whisky glass, then back to me, then back to my glass. His eye then sought out the barmaid's eye, then my glass, and with a nod towards my glass again, some secret code had been passed between himself and the barmaid. She came over, picked up my now empty glasses and said, 'Same again lad?'

'Cor, yeah,' I said, and 'Thank you very much.'

'Don't thank me. I'm not paying for it – the chap along the bar is.' Having said this she took both empty glasses, refilled them, placed them in front of me and went further along the bar for payment from this chap.

I needed to go to the Gents and I would have to pass this man who had paid for my last round of drinks. I stopped as I passed. He made no effort to turn and face me. Instead, my reflection met his gaze in the bar mirror. I said 'Thanks for the drink.' His reaction to this was just a nod and a grunt. I presumed this was bar room jargon for 'You're welcome.'

On arriving back from the Gents, this guy had moved himself onto the barstool next to mine. As I joined him he lifted his glass to me and said 'Cheers.' I did likewise and he began talking to me, mostly about himself. I just listened, occasionally nodding to reassure him that I was indeed listening and that I understood. And the wonderful thing was that I did understand him. He spoke about fear and particularly loneliness. I offered to buy a round but he wouldn't have any of it. As long as I, a fifteen year old boy, listened to him he would buy drinks till the bar called last orders. I felt quite sure of that; it was almost an unspoken agreement between us. By now I knew his name was James, though he preferred Jim, so Jim it was.

'Well, Paul, where will you stay tonight?' He suddenly asked me.

'Jim, you know what, I haven't the foggiest idea!' Having said that I burst into laughter. I was quite drunk and beyond caring where I would sleep. It hadn't entered my mind at all.

'Do you believe in God, Paul?' he asked.

'Yeah, I suppose I do, though I don't really understand where I'm at with Him. By the way, you knew I didn't have anywhere to go; does it show somehow?' I had changed the subject.

'Yes, it shows, lad, least it does to me anyway. Be careful how you go now, won't you. I have to leave you.'

He got down from the barstool, took the first few steps to the door of the bar, then as an afterthought he stopped. His hand made a movement to the inside pocket of his coat. He came back to where I still sat, withdrew his hand and handed me a ten pound note. 'By the way,' he said, 'that God I asked you about – you're going to need Him, if not right now, some day, boy. You can bet your life on it.' Then he was gone from the bar.

I left the bar at closing time and wandered out into the station. I was surprised that although I felt very drunk my legs still carried me quite steadily. I worked out a route on the underground to the West End of London. I'd heard somewhere along the grapevine that Piccadilly was my best bet. There would be others like myself, drifters in this world, looking for whatever.

I left the underground train at Piccadilly and followed the crowd of people towards the exit into the street. I just stood and gazed at the sight of London's West End. People pushed and shoved around me. There didn't seem to be many people like me. They were mostly foreign looking people and most of the chatter that came to my ears was a mystery to me – I didn't understand a word.

I needed to get somewhere where there weren't so many people. I pushed my way through the crowd and veering off to the right I found myself in one of the many side streets. There were no shops; just bars and night clubs with names like 'Whiskey A Go Go'. Most of these places had photographs of near naked females with inviting captions such as 'Lusty Lona' and 'Busty Bertha'. Latin looking characters bragged of the delights to be found beyond the entrances of these places. I watched one man almost pushed through the entrance of one of these bar-type joints. I thought they must be desperate for customers, and from the photographs of 'Busty Bertha' and company you'd be fortunate to come out in one piece. These bars were commonly known throughout the West End as 'clip-joints'. A likely looking punter would be hustled across the threshold, usually someone lured to the entrance by the sight of naked flesh in the photographs displayed. Once inside they would be charged an entrance fee, then charged another fee to enter the bar, then yet another charge before the so-called cabaret started. I wandered aimlessly for a while taking it all in. The drink I'd taken earlier was beginning to wear off: I no longer felt drunk, just groggy.

I found myself eventually in Soho where a shop sign beckoned 'Off Licence'. Like a magnet it drew me to it. I went in, looked at the different bottles on the shelf and selected a cheap bottle of sherry, paid the Chinese-looking man at the till and walked back into the street. I had an urgency to take a swig from the bottle there and then but resisted till I came to Soho Square where I selected one of the benches situated around the Square, sat down and unscrewed the top of my bottle. After taking a large swig I placed it between my feet. One of the other benches was occupied by a lone drinker. At least someone seemed to be where I was at.

I took a few more mouthfuls from the bottle, then I got up and headed for the bench occupied by the other drinker. 'Can I sit with you, mate?' I asked sounding much braver than I really felt. He looked at me, then the bottle in my hand. I guessed that the bottle was my entrance fee into his company.

'Sit down boy. It's a free country so I hear.' He patted the vacant space on the seat next to him.

'You're a bit young for the street drinking crack, aren't ye?' he said in a familiar Irish brogue.

'Is there an age limit then?' I asked, and took another drink almost in defence of my age.

'No, lad, come to think about it, none at all as far as Pat Cahey is concerned. That's myself, by the way, me name that is, Pat Cahey. But there's certain members of the local police at West End

Central that might be thinking differently, if ye get my meaning?'

'Yeah, I do get your meaning, Pat. I hadn't really thought about it. How old do I look then?' I asked him.

He looked into my face. 'You look young, maybe fifteen – am I right? What's yer name, by the way?'

'My name's Paul and yes, I'm fifteen. Here, Pat, have a drink.' I handed him the bottle, he took a swallow and passed it back to me.

'Well, Paul me lad, one thing's for sure, you'll age very quickly on the street. Life won't treat you very kindly, that's for sure.'

He looked at me again. 'But I'd say life hadn't treated ye that well up till now anyhow. And there's a bit of a Paddy in ye, I'd say. Am I right about that as well?'

'Yep, mum and dad both Irish. You're pretty good at this aren't you?' I was beginning to warm to this Irishman. 'How about you then, Pat, how old are you? I'd say about fifty.'

He laughed. 'Remember I said street life ages a man very quickly and if he likes a drop of the hard stuff, even more so. No, me lad, I'm thirtyish, thereabouts anyway. Here, have a drop out of my bottle.'

I told him how I'd come to be in London on my own at fifteen. His was a similar story. He came to England from Dublin when he was sixteen, worked like many young Irish lads mostly on building sites and road construction gangs, and how eventually the drink got the better of him and he just found himself, like me, alone and in London and just the drink for companionship.

'Nobody cares, boy, least of all meself – I'm past

17

caring. Well, I've got about three quid left to me name. What have you got to put towards the next drink, Paul?'

I fished out my money, counted it out and between us we had about ten quid.

'Come on then, me lad, there's an all night deli in Wardour Street with an off-licence. Let's get a couple of bottles to see us through the night. You can doss down with me if you want. How's that sound?'

'Sounds find to me, Pat. You don't mind me tagging along with you, then?' I said.

'Well, me lad, yer fresh company and more important you've the price of a drink and in my world I'll put up with most things as long as there's booze at the end of it, so let's be on our way.'

I spent my first night in London with this alcoholic Irishman. Dossing down with Pat was exactly that, dossing down at the back of a well-known department store in Oxford Street. Pat showed me how to spread layers of thick cardboard between myself and the concrete loading bay which was our bed. Pat disappeared for a minute or two behind a stack of wooden pallets and reappeared with a black bin liner. It contained our blankets. He gave me three. 'Use one for yer head' he said, then 'you'll not be cold here anyhow; there's a heating system of some kind blows warm air under the doors of the building behind us and we've shelter from the rain, with the loading bay's roof. Home from home, lad, eh! Now, let's have a drop of the queer stuff.' I opened one of the two bottles of sherry we'd purchased from the deli earlier, took a swig and handed it to Pat. I sat down on what was to be my bed for the night. Pat sat on his bed.

18

We passed the bottle back and forth, talking about nothing in particular. At one point Pat burst into song. I was not surprised that he had a very good singing voice. Memories of my dad's Irish friends singing in our small living room as I lay upstairs in the bed I had to share with three others came to mind.

What really surprised me is what happened next. He told me to get my blankets wrapped around me and get my head down for the night. We both took one final swallow from the bottle and settled ourselves into our respective makeshift beds. Then the surprise. He started to talk to himself, then I realised not to himself, but to God. The conversation, or prayer, went something like this:

'Dear God in Heaven, I know I'm a pretty poor specimen and my life is a mess, but have mercy on me this night and look after my family wherever they may be, and this young lad here. There's nowt I can do for him but say to you look after him. Good night to yer now Lord, and thanks that even for an auld drunk like meself you went to the cross. Thank you and Goodnight. Amen.'

I lay there for some time and for a while considered that maybe God and this Jesus fella might actually be real, but how, I thought, could they be real for me and for Pat in this condition? No, it wasn't for me. I was quite sure that even at fifteen I was too far gone to start believing in miracles. Damn you, Pat, why did you have to start that praying lark? I realised I'd said this out loud but the only reply I got was the Irishman's snoring. I covered my head with the blankets and sought solace in the darkness. My last thought was of a desire never to see daylight again.

Chapter 2

A Short-Lived Acquaintance

I awoke the next day with my head throbbing – the after-effects of the previous day's consumption of booze. The Irishman was already transferring his bedding into the bin liner. Noticing I was watching him he motioned me with a shake of the bag to do the same. 'There'll be activity around here shortly – we'll need to be away.'

I got to my feet, rolled up the bedding small enough to fit into the remaining space in the bag. Pat pointed to a large industrial refuse container. 'Put the cardboard in that, leave things tidy, me boy.' I gathered up the makeshift mattress and did as he asked.

'What time is it then, Pat?' I asked.

'About seven o'clock, lad. I have a built-in alarm. There's this little hammer goes off in my head telling me my body needs refuelling, and the fuel is there lad.' He motioned to the bottle by a nearby milk crate.

I picked up the sherry, sat on the crate. I took a swig. I had to force it to stay down. My head really hurt now as well. Another swig, then another, the pain in my head subsided, my stomach relaxed.

Pat had found another crate. He placed it by mine and sat down next to me. He was puffing on a hand-rolled ciggy. I handed him the bottle; he passed me the roll-up.

The shutters of the loading bay suddenly rattled into life behind us.

'That's it then, Paul me boy, time to hit the road.' He placed the bottle inside a small canvas holdall that he'd retrieved from the spot where he'd now replaced the bedding. He also handed me a ski-type woollen hat. 'Put that on yer head – it'll age yer a bit.' I did as he told me.

We walked into Oxford Street. It was the middle of September; not a cold day, but autumn was already setting in. We walked about a mile, then somewhere just off Tottenham Court Road we entered a small park. We found a bench and sat down. The bottle came out of the bag. It was soon gone and that concerned me more than anything had for a long time.

'Have we any money left, Pat?' I asked.

Pat produced a handful of coins. 'That's the kitty just now, son, enough for a couple of cans, but I'm sure if you and me goodself put our heads together we'll survive, what do yer reckon?'

'Yeah, I reckon so, Pat,' I answered.

'I'm glad you agree 'cause I'm gonna send ye on a little errand' he said with an impish laugh.

'Now, if you take what's left of the kitty . . . ' He handed me about two pounds. I put this in my pocket.

'Now there's a small Spar Supermarket not far from here, with an off-licence on the premises. Get a couple of cans of lager, the strong ones, and see what else ye can get in that there bag without getting caught. Are ye game, lad?' He looked at me for a response.

'Err, um, well, yeh, all right – I've done a bit of shoplifting before.' I didn't feel as confident as I thought I sounded.

Pat gave me directions to the supermarket. Armed with the holdall for the booty I soon found myself inside the shop. Like a real pro I soon had two bottles of sherry off the drinks shelf along with a four-pack of strong lager secured inside the holdall. I then selected a litre bottle of strong cider to take to the one check-out, which was manned by a lone Asian woman. I was sure that I had been quick enough at my work for her not to have spotted the theft.

I placed the cider by the till for payment. The bag was at my feet. She gave me a few coins in change. I picked up the cider with one hand and almost in one movement, holdall in the other hand, made for the exit. Once on the street I just walked, not daring to look back.

When I was almost back at the park, I stopped and leaned against an advertising hoarding and took several deep breaths.

I undid the cider, my mouth had gone bone dry. I gulped the cider down in thirsty swallows. My arms and legs shook. I had to wait several moments for the shaking to subside.

Then, bottle in hand, I headed back to an eagerly waiting Pat. I swaggered up to the bench, handed him the cider bottle and dropped the holdall at his feet. I really did feel quite proud of myself. The fact that I had just committed a crime seemed unimportant. I felt I'd succeeded for once in my life. The fact that I was a thief actually made me feel good, and Pat would be pleased when he looked inside the bag, which he was doing now.

'Well, praise the Lord! and pass the ammunition. Yer a diamond lad, fair play to yer! Here, have a can.' He passed me the beer. I sat down and sipped at the can. I suddenly realised I hadn't eaten for at least the best part of twenty-four hours.

'Pat, what about grub? We've got the liquid nourishment, what about eating? Not that I'm really hungry.' I added this to my question not wanting Pat to think I was wingeing, or being a wimp.

'I'll show yer all the handouts, in time – don't be fretting about such trivia as food. We've the best nourishment at hand – sherry, cider and beer, otherwise known as lunatic soup.' With that said he knocked his can against mine saying, 'To lunatic soup!' I suppose we are in a bit of a loony situation, I thought. 'Oh, who cares anyway – I'm gonna get stoned, not just now but tomorrow, the next day, the next, maybe till they have to lock me up in the loony bin! Yeah, Pat, here's to lunatic soup and to all the other loonies out there!'

We cracked open one of the bottles of sherry I'd nicked, passing it between us talking crazy drunken talk. Pat had 'the gift of the gab!' It was never certain if he spoke the truth: he probably didn't. A lot of what he spouted out seemed too far-fetched. I too made things up as I went along. The only thing that was for real was that Pat was a seasoned drunk and I was on my way to becoming the same.

I looked at Pat who was swigging first from the sherry bottle, then from the cider bottle. The two cans were finished and now lay in the litter bin nearby.

Pat motioned towards the entrance to the park. Two uniformed figures were making their way towards us – a male and a female. They were soon standing in front of us – a PC and a WPC. 'Top of the morning to yer, officers' Pat said. He suddenly appeared quite sober and collected. I would have to leave this situation in his hands.

'Good morning, Pat.' They knew him.

How's yer good selves?' he asked. Then, 'this here's me nephew, Danny Cahey, keeping me company like. Loner like meself. Needs a bit of cheering up now and again.'

The WPC paid particular attention to me.

'How old are you, then, Danny?' she asked.

'Nearly sixteen, Miss,' I replied, realising I had more or less been honest.

She asked me several more questions. I answered them with lies or half truths. She seemed satisfied with what I'd said. The male officer said something about juveniles and drinking and adults who encouraged under-age drinking. He looked at Pat as he said this. 'But a fine pillar of the community like you wouldn't do that, now would you, Pat?' he asked sarcastically. 'Not at all, Constable!' Pat replied with almost as much sarcasm.

Don't overdo it, I thought. Please God, don't let him get cocky.

The policeman then turned to me. 'If I was you, young man, before you end up like your uncle here, having a permanent relationship with the plonk, I'd think twice before you take another swig from that bottle, do you understand?' I just nodded. There was little point in doing anything else. A blind person could see I'd been drinking. All I wanted was for them to go about their business; catch some real crooks instead of wasting time with us.

At last they were gone, but in no way were they fooled by the story we'd given them about my being a nephew of Pat's. I was convinced of that. I was made aware that my age and my situation could cause problems not just for me but for this Irishman that fate had thrown me alongside. I took a long drink from the bottle. The alcohol dulled the insecurity I was feeling.

Pat meanwhile was cursing life itself. 'A man can't even drink in peace without being harassed. You'd think they had more important matters to pursue – murderers and the like running loose! Me and yer goodself trying to drown our sorrows and only hurting ourselves in the process – to hell with the world and its laws and regulations, that's what I say, me lad. The good Lord must wonder what on earth he created down here. We're victims, lad, not suspects, that's what, we are victims of circumstances. Are we in agreement on that?'

'Yes, Pat, I agree with everything you say,' I replied.

A woman was walking her dog nearby and Pat asked her the time.

She looked at her wrist. 'Eleven forty-five,' she said.

'Come on then, Paul, I'll take you over to St Bernard's Day Centre at Camden. We'll get a meal inside us and a shower and change of clothes. Freshen up a bit, eh?'

'Sounds good to me, Pat. And I certainly could do with that food and a shower sounds pretty good!' I didn't smell too fresh, I knew that.

26

We jumped the train (didn't pay that is) and made our way to Camden Town. St Bernard's was staffed by nuns who we called 'Sister'. I knew this as I'd spent some time in their care as a child.

We joined a group queuing for food, males and females alike, people of all ages, some as young as myself.

We were handed a tray by one of the nuns when we reached the serving area, and sat at a table already occupied by several people. I was in a large Hall. It was very noisy. In between mouthfuls of food, I took in my surroundings. At one end of the hall hung a large wooden cross, which seemed to dominate everything else. Underneath the cross was a banner which read, 'When I was hungry you fed me.'

The food was good – a thick meaty stew with potatoes and a thick slice of bread. I finished what was on my plate. The food had a sobering effect and had been much needed. I felt something like gratitude, so I thanked the cross on the wall: it seemed the right thing to do.

Pat ushered me out of the food hall, across a courtyard to a prefab type building. On the entrance door was written 'Clothing Store'. We went in. A beaming West Indian handed me a bag and told me to help myself to clean clothing which was laid out on trestles. 'Only take what you can fit in the bag,' he said. I selected items of clothing which looked my size and just hoped they would fit.

'Will you be showering then, chaps?' said the black man.

Pat said 'Yes' for both of us. The black man handed us a towel each and a sachet of shampoo. Pat led me through another door, into another

27

connecting prefab which housed the showers. They were extremely clean; I was quite surprised.

I went into one cubicle, Pat into another, where I undressed and showered using the shampoo to wash both hair and body. Pat sang as he showered. A song about 'a wild rover being seldom sober.'

'How are ya doing over there, Paul me boy?' Pat shouted through the partition separating us.

'Just fine, Pat. Thanks for bringing me, I really needed this.' I shouted back.

'Well, just remember where this place is. I won't always be around, you know, and not everyone's as sociable as Pat Cahey.' With that he burst into song again without waiting for a response.

I suddenly remembered my situation and was filled with doubt and insecurity – with no drink at hand to rescue me this time. 'Pat, where's the bag with the drink in it? I could do with a livener,' I called out.

'I had to leave it at the reception area. They have a rule about people bringing bags with booze in them. Ye'll have to wait till we get out, me lad.'

I stepped out of the shower moments later dressed in the clothes I'd selected. I'd been fairly accurate with the sizes, although the denims I'd chosen were a bit loose about my waist. I remedied this by pulling my belt one notch tighter than I would normally have it. The carrier I'd been given now contained my dirty items.

'I don't really want these things, Pat,' I said to the Irishman as he appeared from his cubicle. He took the bag from me, then along with his, dropped them into a large canvas bag hanging from the back of one of the cubicles. 'They'll not be wasted. Probably be washed, ironed and back in the

28

clothing store by tomorrow for someone else to wear – might be yer goodself wearing them again. In this game, you never know!'

We collected the bag Pat had deposited at reception and made our way back to Camden tube and jumped the trains back to the West End. My mind was racing with all sorts of confusing thoughts. Maybe I needed to get away from London and this Irishman with his pretty hopeless view of life, and he had already hinted that he wouldn't always be around anyway.

Arriving at Piccadilly, we sat down under the statue of Eros drinking and watching the steady flow of vehicles and pedestrians passing by. A couple of Japanese tourists took a photograph of us. When they motioned us to look at the camera, Pat gave them a show of two fingers. The Japanese found this hilarious as they clicked away at us with their cameras. Pat got up and went over to them. Words were exchanged, the Japanese nodding vigorously to what Pat was saying. Pat came back and sat down. 'That just cost them a fiver, me lad – never miss an opportunity! Though for the love of Mike I can never understand what on earth they'll be doing with pictures of a couple of drunks. And they think we're mad?'

'Listen lad, I'm off on me own for a while. Do ya think you'll be able to find yer way back to Oxford Street tonight? It's a fairly safe spot, even by yourself. I mightn't get back at all tonight, yer see. What do yer reckon?' He looked, waiting for my reaction. I answered with as much confidence in my voice as I could, 'Oh, don't you worry about that, Pat, I'm a born survivor. Just leave me a drink, and I'll be fine,' then added 'and a couple of quid would help!'

29

'That's me boy, I knew you'd be OK. I'll just get a bit of change across the way.' With that he got up and disappeared into Piccadilly. He never came back.

'Well, at least I've got a drink left; that's something. Not much, I suppose, but better than nothing.' I was thinking out loud. A woman passing by looked at me with pity. I returned her unwanted pity with an angry snarl. She hurried away.

Chapter 3

Birds of a Feather

The last of the drink I'd been left with I shared with a woman. She just came and sat next to me. Her name was Mary. She was a prostitute and also a drug addict. The prostitution supported her addiction, she told me quite openly. I shared with her my story, how I'd arrived in London and didn't have anywhere to go, that I would be sleeping rough again that night. Mary was looking me up and down. She seemed to be making up her mind about something and then she said, 'Listen, Paul, I've got a little flat over the Cross (Kings Cross). Stay for a while if you like – only I don't want any trouble with the old bill or social workers, so you be discreet – in other words, be careful! Do you get my drift?'

'Yeah, I get your drift, Mary. Thanks, I won't be any trouble to you, I promise,' I replied. I felt a great relief. I had somewhere to stay!

I looked at Mary now. She looked a bit undernourished, maybe, but that would be the drugs. She was really quite pretty, about twenty years old, I would say. I asked her ... in fact she was only seventeen. 'Never mind all the questions, mate, I need to make some cash a bit sharpish.'

'Do you know where McDonald's is?' she asked. I didn't, so she gave me some directions pointing in the general direction that the McDonald's restaurant was situated. 'Meet me in there, say about four-ish.' She looked at her watch. 'It's nearly two o'clock now. Try and get something on in the next couple of hours.'

I looked at her, puzzled. She understood my lack of street knowledge. 'I'll put it another way, shall I? Make some bread, you know – money? I'll do my bit: you do yours. See ya.' Then she was gone.

Make some money! How? Steal it, I suppose. Quite simply, go out there and steal it – a voice, not my own, seemed to tell me this. I got to my feet, picked up the holdall and walked into the West End crowds. The booze had made me tired. I really didn't feel like doing much at all, let alone thieving, but somehow I just knew it would decide if I was to have a future where Mary was concerned. After all, she has offered a bed for the night and I would do my bit somehow; I just had to.

I turned into one of the smart-looking side streets off the main drag. This street had several posh-looking small hotels among its dwellings. I went into one such hotel, found myself in a rather plush reception area. I could hear voices from beyond a door situated behind a small bar which doubled as a booking desk. I walked away from the voices to some stairs. A sign at the first step said 'Residents Only'. Glancing behind me I made sure the coast was clear and took the stairs to the first floor. There were doors either side. I stopped at the door with the number 15 on it, and looked up and down the corridor before trying the handle. Crikey! It opened! Slowly I eased the door further ajar. I could now see into the room and could also hear a bath – no a shower – running nearby. I crept into the room and very quietly closed the door behind me. As I quickly glanced around, there were two doors, both closed, to my left, and twin beds against the wall to my right. On one of the beds, male and female clothing, taken off in a hurry by the look of it, was just strewn across the bed. I could hear muted voices from beyond one of the adjoining rooms. I wanted out of here quickly. There was a handbag on the bed. I stuffed it into the holdall, along with a pair of trousers and a man's blazer. There was a small bedside cabinet between the beds and on it was a watch, some rings and a small purse. All went into the bag. Then I was moving towards the door silently to make my escape. I stepped into the corridor, took a really deep breath and walked as casually as I could towards the stairs. I descended to the reception foyer. There was activity around the booking area. Nobody gave me a challenge or even a second glance. What a cinch, I thought!

Back in the crowds of Piccadilly, I felt safe. I went a few hundred yards further into Leicester Square and descended into the public lavatories. I let myself into one of the cubicles. Safely locked in, I sat on the loo and exhaled a great sigh of relief. I'd got away with it!

I retrieved the handbag from the holdall. Opening it gave me a thrill. There was a large purse concealed within the different pockets of the bag. My fingers trembled as I opened it. Bingo! There was a wad of crisp assorted notes, over two hundred pounds! I was amazed at my luck. There was also a handful of silver, an expensive-looking gold pen, a gold lighter, passport, driving licence and a cheque book and several credit cards. Now I pulled the trousers out, went through the pockets, found some loose change and some keys. The keys went into the handbag to be dumped. Everything else I put back in the holdall. I took the blazer out next. In the inside pocket I found an expensive gents wallet and inside another jackpot – about a hundred and twenty pounds in ten pound notes. I shook with excitement. Boy, oh boy! I needed a drink to calm me down. It was too much! Anything I wasn't going to keep I placed on top of the blazer, rolled it up into a ball, then using the trousers as a cord, tied the lot together. Then I stuffed the bundle behind the toilet and got out of there and back into the street. A clock in the Square told me it was 3.45. I needed a strong drink, picked out a ten pound note from the booty, found an off-licence, purchased half a bottle of Bells and headed for McDonald's.

I ordered a large coffee and a quarter pounder and sat myself at a corner table. I took the half bottle of Bells from the holdall and without anyone noticing, poured a generous measure into the coffee. I lifted the coffee carton to my lips with a slightly shaking hand. I drank, then drank again and relief flooded through my jangling nerves. Slowly, I gained composure. I ate the hamburger hungrily, added some more Scotch to my coffee and then just sat back and waited. Mary strolled into McDonald's at about 4.30. She purchased a Coke at the counter and came to join me at the table.

'What you been up to then?' she asked.

'Not a lot really, this and that, you know.' My answer was given with caution. Something triggered alarm bells in my head. I didn't want to tell her how much money I'd made. I wanted to be in control of this situation; it seemed important.

'I've got some whisky if you want to lace your Coke with it.' I passed the bottle to her across the table. She helped herself to a good measure. She took a mouthful, put her drink down and said, 'Made a bit then, did you?' sounding less interested than she really was.

'Yeah, I did a few quid like. We'll sort something out later. Not here though, it's not the best place for it really. Back at your place would be better – that's if your offer still stands – does it, by the way?' I asked. If she says no now, I thought, I wouldn't be that bothered anyway, not with the stash I had in the holdall. It gave me a sense of freedom, and the whisky was by now making me glow with confidence.

She spoke. 'No, mate, the offer still stands. You can stay for a while – till you sort yourself out, that is. In fact, I'll take you over to the Cross now. Let's split now, OK?'

'Yeah, I'm ready – just want the loo first though – back in a tick,' I said. Taking the bag with me I headed for the toilet. In one of the cubicles I took fifty quid from the booty and put it in my trouser pocket. I took a swig from the whisky bottle, allowed it to settle in my stomach and went back into the restaurant. 'Ready, then?' I said as I arrived back at the table. She was already on her feet.

'Yeah, I'm ready; let's go.'

Out in the street she suggested taking the tube to

Kings Cross. I said, 'Let's take a cab – treat ourselves. I'll pay.'

'Last of the big spenders, eh!' then she added 'But if you're paying, let's go for it.'

There was a fleet of black cabs in Leicester Square. We climbed aboard one of them. Mary gave the driver a destination in Kings Cross.

We arrived at Argyle Square about five minutes later. I paid the driver and followed Mary into one of the houses in the Square. Mary's home was on the ground floor. It consisted of a small bedroom, an even smaller lounge and a kitchen. She shared a bathroom which was located on the second floor with the other occupants of the house.

'Well, Paul, it's not much but it's home, for want of a better description. I never bring customers here. Far too many weirdos in my game, so I have them take me to their homes or hotels. I never let them know where I live. A girl's got to have some privacy after all, hasn't she?' She spoke about selling herself as if it was quite normal. For Mary I realised now that it was. My heart went out to her.

I was sitting on a two-seater sofa. She sat opposite in an old leather armchair smoking a very large cigarette. From the aroma it produced I knew it was a joint of hashish. 'Here,' she said, 'have a toke – it'll mellow you out.' Then she giggled as she crossed the room to hand it to me. I took several deep drags holding it in as I'd watched her and others do. It made me feel sick but at the same time it caused me to feel pleasantly light-headed. 'This is nice, Mary. Shall we have some whisky with it? I've got some left.'

'Yeah, good idea' she said dreamily. 'You'll find some glasses in the kitchen somewhere.' I handed her the joint back taking a huge lungful before I did. I almost fell as I stumbled towards the kitchen. I had to hold myself up against the sink. The room was spinning and I closed my eyes. A cold sweat broke out on me. Gradually the spinning stopped. I opened my eyes and the sickness subsided. By the time I'd returned with the glasses, I realised that I was feeling what people had described to me in the past as being stoned. I could get quite fond of this, I thought to myself!

I poured the remainder of the Scotch equally into the two glasses I'd brought back from the kitchen. I handed one to Mary and in return she gave me what was left of the joint. I flicked the long ash from the end of the joint into a large copper ashtray which lay on the glass coffee table in the middle of the room. I sat on the sofa, joint in one hand, whisky in the other. Mary had put some music on her stereo. The voice of the singer seemed to come from far off and it seemed to echo in my head. I had never felt as close to another human as I now felt towards Mary, this young prostitute. I decided to tell her about the money and other stuff.

'I'm going to show you something, Mary.' I went for the holdall, which lay on the floor next to Mary's chair. I took all the money and other items out of the bag and placed them on the coffee table. Mary's eyes lit up. She gathered up the jewellery. 'This lot has got to go. Can't keep hot goods around here. I can sell it all tonight when I go to work. I can probably get another hundred for the jewellery. I can sell the passport and cheque book as well – maybe the driving licence too. Can I do that?' she asked.

'Yeah, that's fine by me, Mary,' I answered. Then

I added, 'half the money that's there is yours as well; fifty-fifty, OK?'

'My little knight in shining armour, you're a godsend!' She came over and planted a big kiss on my lips. 'I've got a couple of tricks to turn tonight and need to pick up some dope as well. I'll part-exchange the jewellery if you like; it's one way of getting shot of it. What do ya say, partner?'

She looked at me for an answer. I agreed with her with a nod and a smile, then asked her if there was an off-licence nearby where I could get some beer.

'You just relax. I'll pop out, get some beer and a bottle of the hard stuff. Back in a jiffy.' Then she was gone.

I got up from the sofa. My legs felt a little like they might not want to carry me. Mind over matter, I thought, as I put one foot in front of the other. They were working a little sluggishly, but working. I had a look in her bedroom. Strange – two beds, not one. I pulled open a drawer of a dressing table. It contained among other things disposable syringes. She must be injecting her drugs, probably heroin. A scary sensation went through my body. I thought how fond I was of alcohol, how I needed a drink even now. In a very short while alcohol seemed very important to me, more important than anything else. I went back to the lounge to await Mary's return. More importantly though I needed a drink.

Five minutes later, Mary was back with the booze. She tossed me a can of beer from the kitchen. I'm gonna take a bath, then I have to go out.' She was back in the room with me now. Quite unexpectedly, she began to undress in front of me talking about this and that as she did so. She sat down in her chair. She too had a beer in her hand. 'Think yourself very privileged – it costs a bloke a tenner just to see me like this.' With that said, she stood up and performed a sort of twirl. 'What do you think of the goods then?' she asked, mockingly I thought.

'You're very nice, Mary, very attractive, yes, err, um, very sexy.' In fact, I'd never seen a naked adult female, only in magazines passed around the approved school. I guzzled my beer. 'Mary, could I put some music on?' I asked. 'Yes,' she replied, giving me a seductive wink at the same time. I got up from my seat and made myself busy at the music centre. I put on a Stevie Wonder album. When I turned around, she was emerging from her bedroom in a pink bathrobe. 'I'm gonna have that bath. See you in a bit.' She was looking at me as she said this. She delayed for another moment and said, 'Some of us get hooked on drugs, some of us the drink.' Her eyes went to my beer. 'Don't be deceived. That stuff has no respect for age, class or circumstances.' With that she blew me a kiss and went for her bath.

When she came back about fifteen minutes later, she busied herself in her room humming along to the music. I really like this person, I thought. She interrupted my thinking with a shout, 'Paul! Pick up that clobber I dropped on the floor in there, will you, and bring it in here! There's a couple of phone numbers in my jeans pocket that I'm gonna need tonight.'

I did as she asked and took her discarded clothing into her room. 'Just drop 'em on the bed for me, love. By the way – you have a choice – use the spare bed in here with me or the sofa. Now be a real gem and bring me a beer. I'll have that, then I'll have to go. I've already put the jewellery in my bag to do a deal with tonight.'

Nodding my approval, I went for the beer. She'd moved to the lounge from her room. She was fully dressed now and looked very smart in what were seemingly quite expensive clothes. She'd done something to her hair as well and had applied some makeup. She somehow looked quite innocent; certainly not like a callgirl. But I presumed that her appearance was deliberately deceptive, and that the innocence would be appealing to her clients. I thought how quickly I was learning. All of a sudden I didn't want this girl to be what she was. It seemed so cruel that such a pretty, ordinary soul could be a drug addict who survived by selling her body.

'What a good looker you are, Mary!' I said. You could have any man you fancied looking like that, you really could.' I felt myself blushing as I said this.

'Quite the charmer, aren't you, with a few beers in you! But you're nice as well and a good looker,' she replied. 'Now though, it's back to reality and that jungle out there. I don't usually get back until the early hours so crash out when you want to. Just help yourself. I'll have to leave you a key if you want to go out.' She finished her beer and left.

I sat around the flat drinking and listening to Mary's record collection. I got up from the sofa and had a nose about in her room. I found a joint already made. 'She won't mind me smoking this, I'm sure,' I thought.

Back in the lounge, seated on the sofa, I drank and smoked. I'd started on the whisky Mary had brought with the beer, and put some music on.

Someone sang of lonely nights and empty days. I drifted off somewhere. I moved at some time to the ash tray on the coffee table, then back to the sofa. 'Where am I going?' a voice was saying over and over again. My own voice? Who knows, who cares or who gives a damn. Then blackness, oblivion. I passed out.

Chapter 4

Partners In Crime

I was still living at Mary's flat weeks later. I'd now turned sixteen. It was October 1979. I'd taken to sleeping in Mary's room, sometimes in the spare bed, sometimes in Mary's bed. I eventually lost my virginity to this drug-addicted prostitute. Sometimes when she was really stoned she talked dreamily about her past. She cried one night as she told me about her mother and father. Like my father, her father was an alcoholic. He raped her when she was fourteen. I was the first person she had told. She had her first experience with drugs soon after and had drifted into London looking for kicks. She just slept around at first for a meal and a bed. Then she met a wealthy Chinese man who gave her one hundred pounds to spend the night with her but the sex was not straight – it was quite perverted. He in turn introduced her to his friends and business pals, male and female, who also paid her for perverted sex sessions. It was while she was visiting one of those clients that she was introduced to heroin. She had her first fix and became enslaved to it very quickly. The only way now she could earn enough to feed her habit was by prostitution, selling herself almost on a daily basis. She told me about the hundreds of very young prostitutes male and female, many of whom were runaways and lived very similar lives. Some were looked after by pimps, who in return for giving them a safe place to live, took most of their earnings, and used them for their own sexual gratification. Mary rented her flat from one of her clients. She paid in kind rather than with money, which included all her bills, electricity, etc. At least she was free of pimps, who far from looking after the youngsters who came into their clutches more often than not treated them like animals. I was beginning to realise just how easily I could end up far worse off than I was at the moment.

I would spend most days on the street. I stole from shops, mostly clothing and cosmetics which Mary sold when she went out at night. Her heroin addiction was very costly and I also was drinking more and more. I would stop drinking for a day, sometimes two, drinking just soft drinks. My hands would shake during these dry periods. I would soon start again, vowing that I would only drink at night and just a few beers, no spirits. I'd manage this for a while as well, but eventually I would be back to round-the-clock binges. At sixteen I was able to admit readily to myself that I was an alcoholic. I could drink vast amounts of booze and Mary made the comment one day that I must have hollow legs. I never got what one would describe as falling down drunk, except when I smoked dope as well. I would then actually get so stoned that I couldn't stand. I only got like this in the flat: never in public.

The only thing I never shared with Mary was my

43

belief in God. I didn't understand God in a biblical sense, but I just had this strange sensation at times that God was there, and often when Mary was away from the flat I would pray out loud to him to help us both. I realised that the way I was living was wrong – the thieving, the sleeping together and the drinking. I would make promises to this God to stop drinking and stealing and that I would even go to church, but the next moment I would be out looking for something to steal and opening another can or bottle, then I would shelve the very thought of giving up this crazy lifestyle. Besides, God made me this way, so surely it was his mistake, not mine?

One day, Mary announced that we were going to have a visitor. He wasn't a client, just a friend. He arrived on a Saturday morning and introduced himself as Brian. I took an instant dislike to him. He wore a lot of gold jewellery and drove a flashy car. All in all, he was a right Jack the Lad and he kept calling me 'boy' which I couldn't stand. This Brian was about twenty-five years old. He reminded me of a tailor's dummy that had somehow come to life.

That night he took Mary and I for a meal, then on to a club which he apparently owned. Mary told me in his absence that he had once got her out of a really tight spot with some drug dealers and had never asked for repayment of any kind. People like that, she said, were few and far between. He was a career criminal and, yes, he was a bit of a flash Harry, but underneath all of that he had a soft spot for the underdog. Brian had never known who his parents were and had lived in an orphanage until he was fourteen. He had lived as a houseboy for several high class prostitutes. One of those prostitutes died and left him everything she had as a reward for looking after her better than any family of her own had done.

'I must admit, Mary, I hadn't really taken to the bloke, if you know what I mean. Goes to show though, after what you just told me, never judge a book by the cover, eh?' And I meant it.

'Shush – he's coming back!' whispered Mary.

Brian sat down with us. He said that we were to order anything we fancied from the bar. We were his guests and there was no charge.

We left the club in the early hours of Sunday morning. In the car going back to Kings Cross I thanked Brian for a nice evening. I was fairly drunk and so was Mary. Brian didn't seem to drink much, in fact I could recall seeing him only once with a glass in his hand and that may well have been a soft drink for all I knew.

He dropped us off at Argyle Square. As I was getting out of the car he handed me two ten pound notes and a card with his phone number on it. 'Give me a buzz tomorrow morning mate. I might have a job for you, if you're interested. Know what I mean?' he said with a wink.

'Yeah, I'll do that, and thanks for this,' I indicated the twenty pounds in my hands. He then said 'Take it easy mate, you've a fondness for the booze I've noticed. I'm not preaching or anything but there's more to life you know. See yer.' Then he sped away leaving me alone on the pavement.

When I arrived in the flat Mary was conked out on one of the beds, the tools of her addiction on the bedside table. She had just had a fix. I took the quilt off the other bed and laid it over her carefully. She moved slightly and mumbled. It sounded like 'Thank you.' I bent down and kissed per perspiring cheek. 'See you in the morning – or later, more like – it is morning now! God bless.'

I took a blanket with me from the spare bed and headed for the sofa in the lounge. As I went to close the bedroom door, she said quite clearly, 'Who's he?' Nothing else – just that.

A while later, I lay on the sofa and also asked the same question to nothing and no-one in particular. 'Yeah, just exactly who are you or what are you?' I wasn't expecting a reply and I never got one. Very soon I fell asleep.

Chapter 5

Into the Lion's Den

It was about a week later that Brian called at the flat. It was unexpected, he just arrived about nine o'clock in the morning. I'd been drinking heavily the day before and was feeling very shaky. I remembered that two cans of strong lager remained in the fridge. With those inside me I might be able to face the day. Nine o'clock was not really early to start drinking, not for me, anyway. Recently, I'd often woken as early as four in the morning, sweating, shaking, heart pounding, needing desperately to get alcohol in my system. I believed that by now I was caught up, ensnared, trapped in this alcohol-induced hell. The only means of making this bearable was the deluded understanding that the demon alcohol itself would bring relief. I was a slave to the wretched stuff. There was, it seemed, no way out. It had mastered me.

Brian was here now seated with me on the sofa. He watched me as I gulped the beer down. 'You are in a mess mate,' he said. 'I really don't like to see a young man with so much potential going to the dogs. I'm gonna straighten you out, make you somebody, starting today. How's that sound?' He looked at me cunningly. I thought 'he thinks I'm a mug. What's he after? He couldn't care less about me, but I'll play along, see where it leads.'

'Does my drinking bother you Brian?' I asked. He replied in a patronising tone that it didn't bother him as such, but that he needed me today. 'In fact,' he said, 'I'm relying on you, you're my main man today.'

Emotionally I had several different feelings about this statement. My ego was thrilled that I might actually be of some use to this man, in whatever way. In many ways I did actually like him; trust him, never, but yes, I liked him.

Any relationship I took on with this bloke was going to end with big trouble, but I was already in a mess, I thought.

I was on my second can. Brian was in the kitchen now chatting with Mary, the sound of cups rattling, water running, just normal kitchen sounds. The beer was doing its job, relief was coming.

Brian came back into the room and sat with me again. He sipped at the coffee he'd brought in with him.

'Get yourself cleaned up then, Paul. Time to prove yourself. You can finish your beer, but I want you to promise you'll gather your wits together. I've got a job for you, in fact I'm relying on you to keep sober till the work's done. Do I have your word, mate?' He offered me his hand. I took it and promised. My fate was sealed with that hand shake; I'd entered some form of criminal conspiracy with this man.

We left the flat together, Brian and myself that is, and got into his car and headed out of London into suburbia. We drove for about an hour. We parked in a tree-lined avenue, with large houses situated either side of the road. Prosperity loomed all around. Brian pointed out one house. I could see it quite clearly from the passenger seat of the car. 'That house, I've been informed from reliable sources is unoccupied, Paul, and in one particular room a fair amount of cash in just waiting for you to go and collect it.' Then he quickly added, 'You're game, aren't you? Not scared surely. I'm relying on you, you realise that don't you?'

He then told me the layout of the house, particularly the room I was to concentrate on.

'I'll go and do it, then' I said. I got out of the car. I felt almost hypnotised as I walked shakily and with a lot of fear along the gravel pathway, making my way to the rear of the house. I approached some bay windows and peered through one of the windows. The room I saw was unoccupied. The lock inside protruded and a key stuck out from it invitingly. I found a rounded stone on one of the flower beds, picked it up and aimed it towards the pane of glass nearest the lock. The glass shattered. Without hesitation I reached for the key, turned it in the lock and seconds later I was in. I was trembling with fear and also excitement. There was no turning back. I looked around me. Affluence such as I had never seen before! 'Get on with it, Paul!' I said out loud. I made my way upstairs to the bedrooms. I found the room I was to concentrate on with a large bureau in it. This is it, I thought, this is where I'll find the money. The bureau was locked. Back downstairs I found a screwdriver in a kitchen drawer. I quickly dealt with the lock. I was a natural at this, I thought. I searched the bureau quickly – I wanted out of there as fast as I could. A black cash box was my first find. It also was locked; no time to mess with it now. I looked around the room. A sports bag on top of the wardrobe – just what I needed! I grabbed it down, unzipped it, dropped the cash box into it, continued searching through the drawers of the bureau. A wad of notes in one, foreign currency in another, jewellery in yet another, more notes and so on, until I'd checked every nook and cranny.

Enough! I had an urgency to get out. I realised I was trembling from head to foot. I half ran, half stumbled down the stairs. I stopped, put the bag down and took a deep breath. Warm globules of perspiration ran down my face. Then I saw the bar in the room and its array of bottles. Just what I needed more than anything else! I took out a bottle of expensive brandy, took the top off and raised the bottle to my lips. Such relief as it burned its way down to my stomach! After several large swigs, confidence took over. Finger prints, I suddenly thought! ... minutes later I was satisfied I'd wiped every area I'd touched. Bag in hand, I hurried back to the car. I still carried the bottle of brandy in the other.

I clambered back into the car. 'Come on, Brian, get me out of here quickly, get me away from here!' We drove off, Brian's voice reassuringly saying, 'Stop panicking, Paul' and 'Well done! You've done really well' and 'Have another swig if it helps – just pull yourself back.' I drank more brandy, then began to relax.

We stopped at a pub once back in London, somewhere close to Paddington Station, which we passed a minute or two before. Brian brought some drinks – only halves of beer, I noticed.

'Pop into the Gents, Paul, and throw some cold water over your face. Just have a quick spruce up. You'll feel better.' He said this and I just got up and did exactly that. He drank his half pint and told me he was leaving now. He handed me a twenty pound note. 'I'll see you again,' he said. 'Your half will be at the flat, so don't worry. See you soon.' Then I was alone.

I came to in the flat on the sofa. I'd proceeded to get very drunk as soon as Brian had left me in the pub. Mary came out of the bedroom. 'Hello, Mary' I said. 'How long have I been back here?' I asked sheepishly.

'You fell through the door about an hour ago. What a state you were in: quite a celebration you must have had!' Then she laughed.

'Why are you laughing?' I asked. 'I feel awful. I can't see anything funny about all this. I think I'm dying' I added.

'No, you're not dying, Paul! This should revive you if that's the case.' She tossed a large brown envelope into my lap.

'That's yours. Brian left it. He said he'll see you again soon.' As she said this she turned and went into the kitchen leaving me alone.

I opened the envelope with shaky hands, tipping the contents into my lap. Over three hundred pounds! In my mind I saw rows and rows of bottles – that's what it represented! I placed the wad of notes back inside the package. I was suddenly overwhelmed by a wave of fear – the realisation of what had taken place.

Had I wiped every print away? They had scientists who worked for the police nowadays. Brian was all right; his prints had no chance of being found as he didn't come in with me. I was the culprit they were seeking. 'Oh, crikey,' I said out loud. Then 'Mary! Mary!' I called. She came out of the kitchen. 'What's all the excitement about? What's up? You'll give yourself a heart attack!' she exclaimed. 'I'll get you a drink.' She brought me some cans of strong lager. 'Just have a steady drink and calm down. Everything is under control, OK? I'll put some music on – Pink Floyd.' Minutes later someone was singing about being 'comfortably numb'. The music and beer began to work. Why was I being such a wimp? After all, I never mugged an old lady. Those people could afford it ... serves 'em right leaving all that money and gold lying around.

Mary was back in the room with a tray. She placed the tray on my lap. 'I've heated it up; it's Chinese. Eat it up! I don't want a scrap left, do you hear me?' She was quite serious and I was actually quite hungry. I finished everything on the plate; every scrap. I drank more beer. Then I had a bath. I was feeling more human now. I found clean clothes and put them on. I was rich! It suddenly dawned on me – I was rich!

The rest of that day went past slowly. I was thinking seriously about drinking, how I needed to get it controlled. I was thinking that all that money could kill me if I wasn't careful. 'The root of all evil,' I said out loud. 'Ill gotten gains.' I felt guilty now my conscience told me I was a bad lot. I made excuses for my actions. I was the victim here. Not those I'd taken from – they were probably insured.

They'd get every penny back in time. I thought about confession, those Saturday mornings at St Joseph's, how I spilled out my sins to the shadowy figure behind the grill in the confessional, the relief I would feel on my exit after the priest had granted absolution. Maybe I'd find a church and confess to a priest. He wouldn't turn me in. He wasn't allowed to, was he?

Mary had gone out to get drugs. She'd taken some of the money. She was going to bring food and drink back as well. I didn't like being alone with all these thoughts. 'Oh, if there is a God in heaven, please sort this mess out! I don't want to be like this,' I said out loud. 'You made me, yes, you are responsible for this mess, not me. Get me out of it if you're so full of love and compassion.' In that moment, I was quite sure that this time of my life was reaching its climax. It wasn't going to go on. There was trouble ahead and I would just wait for it to happen. Until then, I'd just go with the flow and just hang on in there. Meanwhile, I'd have another beer. When in doubt, have a drink and another and another – who gives a damn anyhow!

Chapter 6

Here Today, Gone Tomorrow

Three weeks or thereabouts had passed. A minor miracle had happened as I saw it then. I was still shacking up at Mary's but the drinking was under some sort of control. I'd had a terrible experience one day while attempting to go without booze. I started hallucinating and came face to face with undesirable things, grotesque beings that spoke to me and came at me. Demonic-looking figures would suddenly be snarling and hissing death threats. I lost touch with reality, went to hell or something like it.

Mary couldn't handle it at all. She dragged me to a doctor she knew who was known to have a sympathetic leaning towards alcoholics and junkies. I can't really remember too much about what happened at that clinic. For about three days and nights the nightmare continued and occasionally a ghost-like figure would pop pills into my mouth and I drifted gradually out of that hell back to reality as I understood it to be. Now I was just having a few drinks, mostly at night. The desire physically to drink more was still very strong but I resisted, became determined that I wasn't an alcoholic. I had cracked it! I was normal, a social drinker in the making, what a relief! And boy, oh boy, what a lie! I was being deceived and that deception would be proved time and time again. Meanwhile I went along with it.

Brian was on the scene again. With the cash I'd saved from keeping the drinking under control he had encouraged me to buy some clothes and other personal items. Mary meanwhile was still spending quite a bit on cannabis and heroin. I also was smoking cannabis quite often. Brian and Mary both reckoned that the dope with just a few drinks was just right for me!

Brian was taking me off for a couple of days. He had fixed up a few jobs and assured me I'd come back with no regrets although he said, 'If you really want to give it a miss, I'll find another partner.' (Another mug, I thought, that's what he really means.)

So, a couple of days later, we set off, again heading out of London. This time we went through North London towards Hertfordshire.

That morning we broke into three properties, Brian actually entering the premises with me. I must admit I wasn't so scared this time. Brian even allowed me a shot of whisky from a bar in one of the houses. Brian took control of all the stolen goods including any cash. I knew he was taking the lion's share but after all as he had told me 'I've got the aggro of fencing it.' He made it sound a real task to do this 'fencing' (selling stolen goods).

We had been away from Mary three days. More break-ins came about. These were not planned, but Brian said he felt lucky. At last he said after one quite successful raid, 'that's it mate, work over.' We had been staying at a small but very comfortable hotel a few miles from where we were operating. 'I'm going to leave you here for a few hours while I get rid of everything. There's a guy in Harrow who's gonna take the lot. Then back to London. How are you feeling anyway?' he asked. 'Oh, pretty good, Brian, pretty good' I answered.

Soon he was gone. I left the hotel and found a supermarket with an off-licence, purchased six cans of strong lager and took them back to the hotel. I lay on one of the single beds and waited for Brian's return from Harrow. I drank beer and listened to the hi-fi provided by the hotel management, then I must have drifted off to sleep. I was awakened by the sound of Brian's voice, 'Wakey, wakey, Raffles' he said.

'Raffles? Who's Raffles?' I murmured. 'What are you going on about?'

Brian tried to explain. 'Raffles was a Victorian kind of Robin Hood – you know, sort of robbed the rich to feed the poor. Well, he probably gave a bit to the poor, but he never made it public or anything. Get my meaning?'

'To be quite honest, Brian, I don't know what or who you're going on about, but he sounds all right, whoever he is or was. I'll stick at just being Paul; I have a big enough problem working me out.'

'Yeah, I know mate. I tell you what – I'll have one of those beers with you, then we'll shift, get back to the smoke, OK?'

'Yeah, OK. By the way, how much did we make? I was thinking maybe I'd like to give it a miss after this.'

I didn't know if I really meant that, I thought as I

56

said it. Brian's answer came back so quickly it took me by surprise.

'Actually, Paul, you can leave right now. Here's your share for today plus what was left of your cash that Mary was keeping. She's kept a bit for expenses. There's a suitcase with the receptionist downstairs with your personal things in that you left at the flat.' He then handed me a card with just a number on it, no name or address. 'Ring that number sometime if you run out of cash, which you will. Just ask for me. Now I've got to shoot off.' He went to leave me. Then, as an after-thought just before he went out of the door he turned, looked at me and said, 'Mary says you'd be better making your own way now, if you, err, get my meaning. See you then, mate.' Then he was gone, just like that.

People seemed to come in and out of my life like Jack-in-the-boxes.

I opened another beer, and thought about what had just happened. Was I scared? No, I thought, scared of what? Angry? No, not angry either.

I had plenty of money, some decent clothes, not much else, I thought, but it was a start.

I left the hotel an hour later, hailed a cab and had the driver take me to Watford. I found a room to rent in a house near the town centre. I paid a month in advance. The landlord was a sharp-faced individual, Polish by the sound of his voice.

'I don't bother you,' he said, then added, 'if you don't bring me bother to my house, OK? That way we good friends. Just pay rent, keep clean room. My name is Stanley. What I call you? Ah?' This was all said in broken English.

'My name is Paul, Stan. Thanks for the room' I said.

'You have work, Paul?' he then asked.

'No, I . . . um, I'm a student. College in London. Err, biology and chemistry.' This sounded about right. It was the first thing that came to mind in answer to his question.

He handed me some keys and explained that one key fitted the front door, one the pantry space in the kitchen allocated for my room, which was room two situated on the ground floor. He gave me one final look up and down, seemed satisfied with what he saw and left me to it.

I unpacked what belongings I had, mostly clothing. There was limited provision to hang things so it was good I only had what I'd arrived with. I had a radio of good quality, a battery-operated alarm clock, electric razor (even though I only needed to shave about once a week, and then just a few hairs under my nose).

There was a sink in the room, and a small cabinet screwed to the wall in front of that. I put toothbrush, toothpaste and other toiletries in the cabinet.

Satisfied with my efforts, I sat down in the one armchair provided and opened the last of six beers I'd purchased earlier. I slowly drank the beer until it was finished. The radio was playing – some bloke talking about the music charts and that we mustn't miss a certain show that evening. Then suddenly, it went dead. The light had been on and that had gone off too. This is a good start, I thought. I got up from the chair and went out of my room into the hall. The light was on out here. Must be a fuse or something. It suddenly dawned – I didn't know anything at all about fuses or electrics.

Somebody came down the stairs. It was a woman. She saw me. 'Hi, just moved in, have you?' she asked. 'Looking for someone or something?'

'Actually, my lights and things seem to have gone off. Everything seems to be all right out here though. Must be a fuse' I exclaimed.

'More likely you need to feed your meter!' she said. 'Let's take a look.' She ushered me back into my room. She pulled my small single bed away from the corner of the room it nestled in. Fixed to the wall was the meter. 'Two bob or ten pence as they are called now, and hey presto! Let there be light!' she said.

'Thanks a lot. As you may have noticed, I'm a bit green about living in bedsits but thanks a lot for your help. What's your name? I'm Paul.'

'I'm Sally,' she replied. 'And now I must get going. People to meet and that sort of thing. I'll see you around no doubt, and err...,' she looked around my room before finishing the sentence, 'Good luck with bedsitland. See you around.' Then she was gone.

I found some coins, put them in the meter. The radio came back on and the light. I was missing Mary. I loved her in a childish kind of way, although it was really another dependency. Dependency was really, like addiction, part of my nature. But I wasn't an addict any more, was I? I mean, look at today, yeah, a few beers – so what! I'd cracked it. I was in charge of the booze now. Those experiences I'd been through, they were just a warning. Now I'll get on with life. When this money I've got runs out I'll get a proper job, make the right kind of friends, really go for it. Meanwhile, I'll have a good time, starting now.

I left the bedsit that evening with the intention of having a good time. I took £30 of the money and hid the rest inside the mattress. I had to make a cut in the mattress to do this. I felt sure that the landlord wouldn't be looking at my mattress for damage. I'd paid my rent: that should be enough. I had no intentions of causing problems for him or for me.

I went to a pub in North Watford which I knew my father used. I'd have a drink with him and his Irish friends. The public bar was crowded. Groups of labourers and their subby (sub-contractor) bosses drank together, in working attire, concrete still clinging to their boots and other clothing. They were loud in drink, threatening even to anyone who didn't know their ways. I felt at home with them.

I found my dad sitting with a group of gypsies. I joined them after ordering a pint.

My dad was drunk – was he ever anything else? 'All right, dad, how's the crack?' The Irish in me would come out now surrounded by this crowd. There were no questions being asked about where I'd been or where I would be going. You were here today and gone tomorrow. I felt with this lot 'easy come; easy go'. My father and I didn't really know each other as father and son, but I knew we were friends; that was important.

'Give us a song, Jim' a voice raised itself above the others. My father rose to the request, ever the proud paddy. 'Give us Kevin Barry' another shouted as my dad stood making his mind up what song he would sing.

Kevin Barry it was, a rebel song, well known by these men.

As I listened it brought back memories of my dad and his friends singing similar songs late into the night, at home. I wondered if dad was remembering the same.

The whole bar exploded into applause and cries of 'up the Republic.' If you had problems with these people, about the political or religious followings that they might have, this night was a night you would be wise to keep the problem or argument to yourself, unless of course you fancied a stay in hospital with a broken skull, or even worse. No, it was safer to be one of them, or at least to appear so.

By chucking out time just a handful of customers remained, my dad and I among them. We'd moved to the bar, dad and I. Dad was in some drunken way trying to tell me he was sorry about the way our lives had turned out, that he had never wanted us put into any children's home, that he could have coped with or without my mother.

'Look, Dad,' I said, 'it's water under the bridge.'

'Water under the bridge, is it?' he said, then looked straight into my face. He was angry but unsure about what to say next. Then he said almost bitterly, 'I don't even know how old you are now, don't even know your date of birth! What a carry on, eh? What a carry on, son!'

I had one more drink with him, then I decided to leave and get back to my room. I realised I was quite drunk; so was he.

I walked home alone. As I walked, I realised I had no family. If I did, then we were all strangers. Time and circumstances had done too much damage. I wasn't blaming anyone. From the things that troubled my Dad's mind – and there were plenty – and from the look on his face, he was suffering enough. At least I can be his friend, I thought, at least that. In time we might know what it is to be father and son, although somehow I knew it was too late for all that.

Chapter 7

A Saint By Name Only

I spent a lot of time drinking now I was back in Watford. Sometimes with my Dad and different members of my family. We were all discovering that the only real thing we had in common was that we all drank. Apart from that, it was an effort to be around one another. It was most embarrassing. The booze, I suppose, covered a multitude of sins.

I'd seen my mum a few times as well and it was no different there either. We all tried hard but somehow deep down, we were trying to separate ourselves from the past, and each other.

There were even fights after drinking sessions among ourselves, always ending with the shaking of hands and comments made, presumably as excuses, for the previous day's drinking, comments such as, 'what's a good drink without a fight at the end of it,' and 'just a family brawl. As long as no-one gets hurt, what the hell!' So it went on whenever we came together.

As the weeks passed, I began to realise money was running out. I had purchased a few things for the room I was renting: a small black and white TV, a few more items of clothing and a quite expensive watch. The drinking was again getting out of hand. Often I would wake in the morning after a session the night before, and not recall where I'd been or who I'd been drinking with. These blackouts filled me with fear. I awoke one morning to find I had company beside me in the small bed – a girl.

I shook her awake, and she opened her eyes. 'Watcha, mate. What a night that was, eh?' she said, before I could get a word in.

'Yeah, wonderful' I said, as I quickly clambered over her to reach my clothing scattered about the room. I got dressed and she began to do likewise. Who on earth was she? Where had she come into all this? Fate came to rescue. 'You don't remember much about last night, do you?' Then she chuckled before adding, 'Not that much **did** happen, not in there anyway.' She indicated the bed. 'Good grass, though; got any left, by the way? Best I've smoked in a while, I'll tell you, and Mandy knows good weed. Well, is there any left? Paul, you said last night? Is that your real name or what? Last night you were trying to come across like James Dean . . . terrible when you wake up to reality ain't it, Jimmy Dean?' She chuckled again. 'Just give us a few quid and I'll get out of your life; it's no problem.'

'Listen, Mandy, if you hadn't just said your name, I wouldn't even have remembered that. I'm sorry, got pretty well stoned it seems.' I didn't know what else to say. I gave her a few quid, and I'd found a small amount of the grass she'd referred to earlier. I gave her enough of this for a few joints. As she was leaving through the front entrance of the house, she turned and said, 'If you want to try the bed scene when you're a bit more together, I'm in the Red Lion most nights. See yer then!'

Alone in the room once more, I tried to recall the last hours of my life. Bits and pieces came to mind. Figuring it out all that had really happened on the surface was I'd got really smashed and had not been very successful in bed with a complete stranger. No big deal; it happens to all of us at some time, I reasoned. Just put it down to experience, or lack of it.

I counted what was left of the money, putting a month's rent by, which left me with about one hundred pounds. The way I was spending, I'd soon be skint. Then what? 'Worry about that when the time comes, Paul,' I told myself. As the saying goes, 'Tomorrow never comes'.

I left my digs at about 11.30, bought a couple of cans of lager from a corner shop and walked into town. I found some public toilets, locked myself in one of the cubicles and drank the two cans. Feeling a bit more like facing the day, I set about finding some company. It occurred to me that locking oneself into a public loo to have a drink was somewhat odd.

I walked into St Mary's churchyard and sat on one of the ancient tombs. On a bench just a few yards away, three scruffy-looking characters sat together. They were passing a bottle one to the other. One of them had spotted me sitting alone and was heading towards me.

'Hello son, how's the crack?' he asked in the familiar Irish accent. Then, 'we was wondering if a young lad like yourself might have a few shillings to spare, help us on our way like. We're on the road, if you – err – see what I mean.'

'Well, I reckon I know what you mean' I replied. 'Take this.' I withdrew a fiver from my pocket and handed it to him. 'I'd appreciate you getting a few bottles and bringing them back here, and we'll share them, your mates as well,' indicating with a nod towards the occupants of the bench who were taking a great interest in what was going on.

'Right then lad, I'll be back, just you hang on now, I'll not let yer down.' And he scurried off then in the direction of the High Street.

He was back within minutes, carry out in a plastic carrier. 'Two bottles of sherry and a bottle of easy rider. How's that? And, err, I took a liberty, ten fags.' He held them up to show me. Then he sat down on the grave next to me. 'Will I open a bottle son? What'll I start on, the wine or the easy rider? (This group of drinkers had a pet name for cider, thus easy rider, I was able to work that out fairly quickly.)

'Open the wine,' I said.

'Will I call the others over? They'll not come over into a stranger's company unless beckoned. You'll make it easier for them if as I call 'em over, you give 'em a kind of welcoming wave.'

So we did that and they came over and joined us. We gave names to each other, we had a Paddy, he had gone for the carry out, a Kevin and a Sean, all Irish. Paddy was the most talkative, and on discovering my surname told me he knew my father and brothers. He had worked with them on building sites. The one they called Sean said very little and Kevin seemed to be the more intelligent of the three. He just sounded as though he had some sort of education behind his speech.

This was my introduction to the boys on 'The

Green' as they were known in the town. I learned that they mostly 'skippered' (slept rough) around Watford and spent their time stealing and begging to feed their drinking habits. I got to know many more like these three in a very short time. I seemed a bit of an oddity to them because of my youth, but they more or less accepted me despite this.

I was going back to my room drunk most nights now, and had exhausted the last of my cash. The landlord had collected the month's rent and also emptied my electric meter. Now I had started working out how to survive. I managed to get a little help from the Social Security, I told a few lies to get as much as I could but it really only kept me in drink for a couple of days, nothing else.

No way was I going back to London, and although I still had Brian's number I never used it.

'I'll do a few jobs on my own,' I thought one day. It was the middle of November by now, winter was here. I still went to The Green most days, the cold weather didn't seem to be an obstacle to these hardened drinkers, and they always had a drink to share with me when I was skint.

Sitting with Paddy, I drank from a sherry bottle, which was half sherry mixed with cider, I discovered when I took my first swig. Paddy called it a 'box up'. It did the trick, although it certainly was an acquired taste!

Paddy had received his 'no fixed abode' benefit that morning. I asked him to lend me a fiver until the next day. 'I need to go to St Albans to make some money,' I told him. 'No problem, yer were good enough to the likes of us when things was a bit on the dry side.' He gave me the fiver.

I set off with my holdall and a few housebreaking

implements, and catching a bus to St Albans, I arrived in the town, found an off-licence and purchased a couple of cans of strong lager and ten cigs. The fiver was gone, a few pence remained. I had to score today, if I didn't it didn't bear thinking about. I sat on a seat a stones throw from the cathedral and drank my beer. It didn't get me drunk but it lifted me a bit for what I needed to do.

I walked around looking for a target, choosing a bungalow less than a mile away from where I'd been sitting. Knocking and ringing the door bell, I made sure I made enough noise to waken anyone that might be sleeping. Silence. Good, I thought – in and out as fast as I could. Pushing the front door hard with my shoulder near the Yale lock assured me that with a bit more pressure it would give. One more hard shove and the lock went. I only had one floor to concentrate on. I was in and back out in less than ten minutes. I was sure I'd left the place clean of prints.

I walked into the town centre and found a pub, ordered a pint with a bit of loose change I'd pocketed from the job, lit up a fag and gathered my wits together. It was quiet in the bar, just a few lone drinkers and a barman leaning across the mahogany topped bar surface, reading a news-paper.

I had a rummage in the hold-all, an expensive camera, a small amount of gold, about sixty pounds in cash. I was quite pleased with my efforts, but having the camera and gold with me was causing warning signals to go off, 'get rid of goods quickly.' I could hear Brian's voice echoing from a past conversation we'd had.

There was a pay phone on a wall by the bar,

several local taxi firms had cards displayed on a notice board, beside it. I dialled one of the numbers, gave my name as Jones and where I was and the intended destination. The cab would be here in ten minutes, and could I please be in the car park of the pub for the pick up, unless, of course, it rained.

Half an hour later, the taxi dropped me at my digs via a Victoria Wine off-licence where I bought a bottle of sherry and some beers. Sitting in the armchair drinking from the sherry bottle, I considered the gold and camera. Where to fence them? Maybe my dad's local would provide a fence. I'd go there tonight: it was Friday, there would be money around, that was my plan then.

At about 6.30 that evening I had a fish and chip supper purchased from a local chippy, drank another beer and waited for the taxi I'd ordered to my dad's local. My Dad wasn't there but I recognised two of the gypsies he'd been drinking with in the past, sat together in one corner of the bar. Joining them with my drink I sat down and said hello, and asked if my father had been around. This was as a means of starting a line of conversation.

'Your father?' one of them asked. 'Would that be James Halpin yer askin' after?'

'Yes, that's him,' I said. 'Have you seen him today?'

'Yeah, we've seen him,' one of them said. 'He staggered out of here three o'clock this afternoon. Probably sleeping it off.'

'Which one are you? Paul, is it?' the older one of the two asked.

'Yeah, that's right, I'm Paul.'

I had a plastic carrier containing the camera and

69

gold. 'I've got this to sell,' I said, and handed them the bag. They both looked the goods over. 'I'll be back in a tick,' the older man said. He left the pub and took the bag and its contents with him. Fast service, with no questions asked. Good, I thought.

'Will yer take a drink with me?' the younger man said.

'Yes, I will,' I answered. He brought me a large whisky back from the bar and a pint of stout for himself. He was a huge man, the type you didn't tangle with.

'Would you fancy travellin', Paul? It's a great life for a young skin like yourself.' He stared across at me, waiting for an answer. I tossed back the contents of the whisky glass. The whisky warmed through me, making me brave enough to be with this man. 'I'd never really thought about that,' I replied, 'about travelling, that is.'

'Well, if you ever want to give it a try, let us know. We pass through here quite a lot, OK – you'd be welcome.'

'Thanks a lot. What do I call you then?'

He looked at me suspiciously. 'Scaley, I'm known as, like a snake if you see my meaning – that'll do lad, just Scaley, OK?'

Nodding my affirmation, I realised that maybe asking these Irish travellers' names was not the done thing.

The older man was back, and ordering a drink at the bar, came to join us.

'There ye are now young man, put that away somewhere safe; it's a hundred – that's it – no more talk of it. Now, let's be gettin' steamed up' (drunk).

I wasn't about to argue, it happened so quickly. I was stuck for words anyhow, and the stolen goods were no longer my problem. The younger of the two men challenged me to a game of pool. 'Loser buys a round, winner plays Milo; that's me partner, by the way.' I finished up buying the next round and quite a few after that. Then they were leaving. None of us got really drunk that night.

Milo told me if I got hold of any other good stuff the cash would always be there. They wouldn't be moving on for a while, if I wanted to see them at any time I was to come to the pub. It was one of the few pubs where travellers were allowed to drink in the area, he told me. So, I now had my own buyer, my own 'fence' if I should ever do any more jobs, and I would at some time, I was sure of that.

I arrived back at my digs that night happy about what the night had brought about, I had money again for a while, and had a roof over my head. 'I've got a beer or two left somewhere,' I said out loud, just a little nightcap, feeling like someone who really was learning to survive. I drank what was left of the beer and most of the sherry.

Waking at six the next morning in the armchair, with a cold sensation around the lower part of my body, I realised that it was in fact my own urine.

What an ugly, disgusting way to start the day. Thank God I'm on my own. There was a small amount of sherry in the bottle by my feet. I swallowed it down quickly and set about cleaning myself and the chair. It was just an accident – too much drink and a heavy sleep. I tried to console myself, but I was filled with shame. By 7.30 I was out on the street, heading for one of the corner shops that would sell alcohol out of legal hours for an inflated price, of course. Looking for company, I headed for The Green.

That Saturday was spent in the company of Paddy and an assorted bunch of his drinking cronies, including one female, a Glaswegian lass who they called 'The Saint', a name given to her because of the tattoo of the mother of Jesus on her arm. She neither looked nor behaved as her nickname suggested. Her real name was Rebecca.

It had been decided that it was too cold for The Green or graveyard, so we now sat in a derelict house, in one of the ground floor rooms. This was home for Paddy and some of the others just now. A fire blazed in an open fire-place, providing warmth. The fuel was anything that would burn. Most of the timber including doors, floorboards, fitted cupboards from the rooms not occupied by the drinkers was systematically being broken for fuel. Any brass fittings or plumbing copper had found its way to the local scrap-yard and thus converted to booze.

Most of the conversation was being directed by 'The Saint'. Every other word that came out of her mouth was a swear word. She often used Jesus Christ and the Virgin Mary in the most vulgar way too, although I believe she did this in ignorance. I'd heard the same phrases uttered as I grew up even from my own father. It was almost commonplace among the Irish and Scots, especially if they were Catholics.

Everybody present had a bottle or can and there was plenty to spare: bottles of unopened sherry and more cans of beer stood in the middle of the floor. There was no furniture, just soiled mattresses strewn around the floor, used for crashing out on. The toilet was a bath tub in an adjoining room which I'd gone to use when I needed to. Needless to say, it was filthy. I took the fastest visit I'd ever taken and almost ran back to the drinking den.

Rebecca at one point seemed to become aware of my presence.

'Who's that weasel o'er yonder?' she asked, or rather demanded, from no particular individual. 'Come o'er here till I get a look at ye! Come on, hen, I'll no bite ye!' She took a swig from her bottle, then rising to her feet she lumbered over to where I sat with Paddy. 'You'll nay come to me, hen, so here I am!' She collapsed across Paddy and myself roaring with laughter. She had spilt some of her drink and didn't seem very happy about this at all. Her mood changed and she ranted and raved for a while about wasting good drink. She was obviously drunker than any of the men. She spoke at me again.

'Does yer mummy know yer here, son, and drinking as well wi' the likes o' us?' Then she suddenly lunged at my crutch. 'Gonna let Becky make a man o' ye?'

I pushed her away from me. For a moment she raised the half-full bottle as if about to break it across my head. 'Ach, you Sassenachs can nae take a jest – please yersel, ye bam pot!' (nut case).

The other drunks looked on without any real interest. Behaviour like this was obviously commonplace for this woman.

She had lost interest in me now and had gone to join two men on the other side of the room. She was allowing one, then the other, to kiss her and fondle her, oblivious to the onlookers who passed vulgar comments to one another and laughed and jeered at the performance. When they had finished with her they covered her over with a couple of soiled blankets and carried on with the more serious pursuit of getting drunk. In the next couple of hours every man present went over to where she lay and joined her under the blankets.

Chapter 8

A Dry Day

The next morning I awoke, hungover and full of guilt and remorse. The events of the previous day filtered through. I'd behaved like an animal and felt like one. I got out of bed and searched around for a drink. Finding some sherry, I took several swallows from the bottle and realised at that moment I was fully dressed and had gone to bed like that. At least I hadn't wet myself. Small consolation, I thought!

After bathing and changing my clothes I felt a little cleaner, but then thought that I might have caught some disease from the woman ... after all, if that was her lifestyle, who knows where she'd been or who with! Maybe she wouldn't remember, but why should that matter? The problem was that I remembered! Drinking the remainder of the sherry, the guilt began to subside. Compromise took its place. Well – it wasn't rape. She was obviously an experienced female and I wasn't the first, and anyway she led us on, didn't she? And, of course, we were all very drunk. From now on I'd just be more in control.

I went to a pub that morning. I'd picked a place

that would be fairly quiet. My choice of drinking hole seemed about right. After my second or third drink, no more than three or four people were in the bar. At lunchtime, I had a pub meal. Yesterday's drunken orgy still dominated my thinking. She, Rebecca – if she cleaned herself up a bit and had some clean clothing on – could be quite attractive. The truth was hitting home. I liked women like 'The Saint', just as I had liked Mary the prostitute. I began to toy with the idea of looking for The Saint, being somewhere on my own with her, drinking with her. She could come home with me. After all, what she needed was someone to treat her differently. I was young, I know, but I was a fast learner and certainly a survivor. I was strangely excited by the idea. I left the pub in search of this person who was no longer someone I'd witnessed being gang-banged, but a damsel in distress, just as I'd been distressed when I hit the streets of London and Mary had given me refuge.

I went back to the derelict house. There were just two occupants in the drinking den, Rebecca and a man who lay drunk in one corner, dead to the world.

The Saint sat drinking alone on one of the mattresses. If she remembered yesterday's events, she wasn't letting on. She eyed me up and down suspiciously. I felt something like compassion for her. 'I was drinking with you yesterday. We got quite drunk, all of us, didn't we?' I said.

'That's not all ye got, son, was it, eh?' Then she quickly changed the subject. She wasn't drunk yet, that was obvious. 'Don't just stand there! Is it a drink ye want? Here!' She offered me the bottle. It was almost empty. I went over, took it from her and drank what was left.

'Wanna come and have a drink with me? I've got money.' I sounded a bit of a wally, I'm sure, but didn't know what else to say.

'You're just a pup, but yours is the only offer goin', so aye, let's have a bevvy, hen.' I helped her to her feet.

Outside in the street I hailed a cab and headed back to my place via an off-licence. By the look on the driver's face, he was glad to get us out of the cab. This woman really didn't smell too good!

Back in my room, I decided to jump in at the deep end and asked her if she'd like to have a bath. I was sure if she got stuck into the booze it would be hopeless to try and get her to do anything. By now I wasn't so sure bringing her here was a good idea. She agreed quite readily to a bath. I got her clothes sizes from the labels attached to what she wore.

I left her in the bath and just hoped that no-one found her here. Then I went off in search of clothes for her. I was tempted to just steal them but reluctantly paid for a full set of things including underwear. I had taken her other clothes with me and now deposited them in a street litter bin. Hurrying back to the house, I realised I had left her in the house with the booze. This worried me as I'd seen what she was like when drunk. She was still in the bath when I got back. The bathroom was situated on the second floor and I took the clothes up to her with a bath towel. She didn't object to my seeing her naked. 'A treat for you, Becky – is Becky OK – to call you that, I mean?'

'Yeah, Becky's fine. I've been called a lot worse, I

can tell ye. You're Paul if I remember frae yester-day?'

'Yeah, I'm sorry about what happened. I got carried away, what with the booze as well.' And I really was sorry.

'Och, don't fret yoursel' – I'm still in one piece, as you can see. Now lead me to the booze. I'll put these clothes on, downstairs.'

Back in my room I watched her dress, and was really pleased that everything more or less fitted her frame. 'Thanks, you're no a bad lad, no bad at all.' She was almost embarrassed by the fact that I'd given her some clothes.

We spent the day drinking together. I took it easy, not getting too drunk. Becky drank like there was no tomorrow. She told me about her life and her Glaswegian accent got stronger as the alcohol took a hold.

Born one of nine children in the Gorbals of Glasgow, she was the oldest. She was thirty years old. When she was twelve her father raped her while drunk. She had told her mother what had happened. Her mother chose to blame her – a twelve year-old child. From then on she hated both mother and father. She started running away from home and sniffing glue with other runaways. She was placed in care and experienced more sexual abuse from both male and female staff. No wonder she was the wreck of a human being she was now.

She stayed in my room for about a week, then one morning I woke up and she'd cleared off taking most of my money with her. I felt let down but at the same time felt I'd taken advantage of her at that first meeting with her in the derelict house, and saw it as a kind of penance from God. She did come back one evening, sporting a black eye. She was very drunk and slept it off for a few hours. I shared some food with her and she said sorry for ripping me off and if I wanted I could use her body as repayment. My reaction was to give her a few quid, send her on her way and say that I was leaving Watford the next day anyhow. It was my way of saying, 'Don't come back!'

Now I was running out of cash again. I spent a lot of time drinking around the town with the down-and-outs. I was shoplifting almost on a daily basis to keep up with the demand for booze.

After one quite successful shoplifting spree in a well-known department store, I decided to take the electrical goods I'd stolen to my dad's local. I had enough to buy a few drinks and a packet of fags, which left me more or less skint.

My dad was there that night. He'd had a win on the horses, so when my money had been spent, he treated me to a drink.

'What are yer wanting the gypo's for, son?' I'd told him I was wanting to see Scaley and Milo.

'Some stuff I've got that they might be interested in.' I indicated the box beneath my feet.

'Nicked gear, I suppose. You watch yourself now, or it's in prison you'll be spending Christmas. You'll not do much celebrating in there, I'll tell yer!' His tone of voice was in warning, not that I shouldn't be a thief: just that I needed not to get caught.

The travellers came in just before closing time with several other men. It was Scaley who came over to me. 'How's the crack then, Jim, and yourself, Paul? Will yer have a drink before last orders?' We both said we would and drinks were bought.

Scaley hadn't missed the box beneath my feet, of that I was quite sure.

'Will I get Milo to have a peek in the box, lad? It's getting late and we need to be shifting soon.'

'Yeah, please do,' I agreed.

Milo just as before was beckoned over. Scaley handed him the goods and he disappeared through the bar door with the box which contained a hundred pounds' worth of goods. If they gave me fifty, I'd be satisfied. I was given thirty-five. A little disappointed, I accepted – didn't really have a choice anyway, that's the way it was. They bought us another drink and left dad and myself together. Time was called. I went back to dad's home. We both felt uncomfortable sitting in the living room of what should've been a family home, but both of us knew in our hearts that too much had happened here. We both felt lonely. Dad told me of his regrets that mum was gone, that he had bumped into her a couple of times and had tried to get back together. Mum had another partner now, he told me, and didn't blame her for keeping away. Several of my other brothers, in gaol for fighting, wrote letters to him. It was quite clear that my dad was heartbroken and very lonely. He said I should stay the night.

He retired to his bedroom saying if I wanted to sleep in one of the other bedrooms, I could. Those rooms held unhappy memories for me so I declined the offer and said I would make do with the sofa. Once I heard my dad snoring I let myself out of the house and walked home, tears streaming down my face.

It was the last day of November, 1980. On rising that morning, I decided I would have a dry day – no alcohol at all. Feeling sick and shaky, I went to the nearby supermarket and purchased several large containers of fruit juice, passing the wine and spirits. The compulsion to buy alcohol was overwhelming. Sweating and shaking by now almost uncontrollably, I made my way to the checkout. The girl cashier looked at me as I attempted to pay for the juice, my hands trembling as she took the money from them. 'Are you all right, mate? Got a fever or what? You do look rough!'

I grabbed my change from her hand and almost ran out of the store, dropping most of the change in the process.

Back at my room I sank into the armchair. My heart was trying to leap out of my chest. I was dying, I thought. There was a knock at the door. 'Yes, who is it? Come in – it's not locked,' I almost croaked. It was the lady from upstairs. 'Hi there, I've been up north for a while; wondered if you might have taken a parcel delivery for me. I was expecting, you know, mail order sort of stuff.' She looked at me hopefully.

'No, I – err – haven't. Don't spend a lot of time in. Really sorry – err – can't really help. Nice to see a friendly face, though,' I rambled. ('Go away,' I was thinking, 'Please go away.')

'You really look stressed out, love, see a doctor if I were you. Tell you what, I've got some mild tranquillisers that might help. I don't need them these days. I'll fetch 'em for you. Just follow the directions on the bottle. You'll be right as rain in no time.' She left the room. I hadn't said yes or no to her offer of tranquillisers but let her fetch them just the same.

She came back with the pills and gave them to me

saying, 'Only take the three prescribed per day. See ya, then – oh, and by the way, they'll help with the shakes as well,' she threw into the air as an after-thought closing the door behind her.

I took two of the pills and longed for them to work. I was tempted to take more, wanting desperately to rid my body of the awful withdrawals. From the very depths of my being I was crying out to a distant God for help. An hour later the shaking had at least subsided. I crawled into bed, first taking another pill. I slipped into a nightmarish sleep. I jumped awake several times in panic, a panic I couldn't explain. Somehow I had to hang on. Sleep again, dreaming of being chased through a laby-rinth of dark rooms, never looking back to see who my pursuer was, just aware that if I were to stop running, something terrible beyond all under-standing would happen to my person. Then – an awareness that if I could wake it couldn't touch me. Somewhere in my subconscious soul or spirit, a childhood vision of a chapel in the Convent, a little boy kneeling, talking to the man on the Cross. 'Say it, say it!' a voice was pleading. 'Say what?' my own voice, my own soul responded. Again the little boy looked up at the man on the Cross, fear on his tear-streaked face – the child's face, that is.

'Please help me, Jesus!' Please help me Jesus! Pleeeeaasse helllpp mmmeeee, Jesus!' I was almost catapulted awake, aware that I'd been actually mouthing that plea for help. Now as I lay awake, a different kind of fear was present. This was a fear that told me I could no longer doubt 'a' God existed and that the Guy on the Cross had a great deal in common with God. At that moment in my life, something very deep had occurred that left me

actually believing that there was more to my existence than just a mere coincidence or act of fate, and
that if I really so desired, I could play a vital role in
changing what was happening to me. A decision
needed to be made at some stage. I wasn't quite
sure what this meant, or rather, something was
blocking my realisation of what that decision was.

I drifted in and out of sleep for the next twenty-
four hours. Finally, half way through the following
day, I ventured out onto the street avoiding the
places where I might be confronted with the real
temptation of drinking. Cruising in and out of
cafes, drinking several mugs of tea or coffee in
each, I still toyed with the idea that I could take a
drink and not get into the same mess as previously.
But for now I was somehow managing to resist.

Almost a week later, complacency set in. It was
just a figment of my imagination, I reasoned.
Though not really believing that line of thought, at
the same time I really wanted to take in the lie
which it was. Having some cash left I bought a
bottle of vodka, drank it, or most of it, and decided
to do another break-in. This time I got caught and
was about to face the consequences.

Chapter 9

Remanded In Custody
(or If You Can't Do the Time,
Don't Do the Crime)

Opening my eyes and focusing them on the concrete ceiling, it didn't take me very long to realise I was in a cell. Recalling to memory what had taken place hours, or was it days, before. I wasn't really certain. The fact was I'd been arrested. The house I'd chosen to rob appeared to have no visible alarm system – but it had. That's right, I remembered now – helping myself to the drinks cabinet in a downstairs room, I had simply made myself at home, a blurred memory of attempting to cook a meal in the kitchen, then the door crashing open and a large male figure rugby-tackling me to the ground, the police. I was picked up on the job.

My thoughts were interrupted. A key was turning in the heavy cell door. A uniformed police officer stepped into the cell. 'Are you sober enough for CID to interview you now, Halpin?' he barked. Shakily I got to my feet, my head thumped and I felt sick. I just nodded meaning I was ready to be interviewed, I really didn't care. They can do what they like, I thought, who gives a damn anyhow.

The CID interviewed me for about three hours, during which time I admitted all the other house-breakings committed prior to the one I'd actually been caught on. I decided to come clean, hoping that I might get probation. At one point one of the officers said that they knew someone else was involved and would I give that person's name. I refused. 'In that case you'll go down on your own. If you want to be a hero, that's your choice, that's OK by us. You see Paul, you're just an amateur, and it's obvious that someone out of your league put you up to most of these jobs.' He looked at me wistfully. My eyes met his and they said everything. I'm saying nothing else. 'Is there anyone you wish us to inform that you are here?' one of the men asked.

'You could tell my Dad, I suppose, although a fat lot of good that'll do.' I gave my Dad's address to them.

They took a lengthy statement from me. Most of it seemed about right, although I was willing to admit someone was with me most of the time. I lied, telling them he had been a man who I'd met on the streets in London and that he called himself Sydney. Then I was formerly charged, photo-graphed, and fingerprinted and taken back to the cells.

The rest of that day and night was spent on a hard wooden bench which doubled as a bed, with one small, thin smelly blanket provided to cover myself with. At one stage during that night I had to ring for the gaoler. I went into very serious DTs (delirium tremens), a police surgeon was called in and I was thankfully heavily sedated for the remainder of the night. Fitfully waking and sleeping, I again began calling out to God for help. 'Sometimes God takes a long time to answer, especially when our hearts are not right with him.' This sequence of words seemed to fill my head almost audibly at one particular waking moment of the night. It left me feeling convinced that if I was trying to fool the creator of this world then, boy oh boy, I was a real sucker. Then morning finally arrived.

Before being taken up to court I was allowed to wash and comb my hair, and was also given medication which the police surgeon had left for me to take, to ward off another attack of DTs.

Standing in the dock of the court room, the charges were read out to me. Scanning the court room I hoped my Dad might have shown, but no. I was alone.

'You will be remanded in custody for twenty-one days,' the magistrate said. The duty solicitor thought this would probably be the outcome – this, he had told me, would enable social workers and such to compile reports about me which should be beneficial when it came to sentencing.

I was led back to the cells, and once more the door banged shut. Fear crept into my mind. Where exactly was I being remanded to? Would I know anybody? Pacing up and down the cold concrete floor of the cell, I had an unreal belief that the heavy steel door would open shortly and the gaoler would tell me I was free to go. Then reality would hit home and I knew that for now I had been removed from the real world. I was yet to find out how long that would be for.

I cursed God for doing this to me and in another mind begged and pleaded with him to get me out of this mess, promising never to do anything wrong again. Finally I could no longer contain my despair, throwing myself down on the wooden bed I cried. No, more than that, I wailed from deep within. I wailed till I could wail no more. Then anger took over. I brought my fists down on the wooden structure of the bed, bang! bang! bang! The noise reverberated around the grim graffiti-marked walls of the cell. I thumped and thumped until finally my bones actually threatened to break. Willing myself to be still, I breathed in deeply and took control of my mind. 'You need to survive this, Paul!' This I spoke out loud to myself. It brought a sense of hope into my situation. Physically I was in a cage, but the will for my mind to stay free was never more important than now.

A probation officer was allowed into the cell. He took some details of my circumstances – where I lived, about my family background, etc, etc. He said he would get my few possessions from my digs and keep them safe. The police had already been there, he told me. It was part of the procedure. My biggest fear was that Brian's phone number was written down somewhere in that room. Had they, the police, found it? I shrugged off my concern for Brian and made up my mind that putting myself first was more important if I was to come though this: everything and everyone else was secondary.

The probation officer had gone. I was alone for about another hour, before again the gaoler came in.

'Get your shoes on then, Halpin. Transport's arrived, you're off to Ashford Remand Centre.'

There were three other prisoners. We were handcuffed in pairs and led out of the cells to a waiting
'Black Maria', otherwise known as a 'Meat
Wagon', the prisoner I was handcuffed to informed
me. Once on board the handcuffs were removed and
we were ushered inside separate little boxes and
locked securely in. There was just room to sit,
although in an extremely cramped position.

The van began its journey. In the box I was in,
there was a small smoked glass slit for a window. If
I strained my neck upwards I could watch the world
passing by, couples hand in hand, seemingly not a
care in the world. We passed a greengrocers quite
slowly at one stage and I could actually see an old
lady selecting individual items from a colourful
fruit display. Just a very ordinary everyday action
by another human, but a deep longing to be doing
that simple thing penetrated deep within. I cried the
rest of the way to Ashford.

The reception area of the remand centre was the
human equivalent of a cattle market. There were
several cages situated around the main processing
area that were crammed tight with prisoners. What
shocked me about the whole thing was that these
young human beings were actually laughing and
joking with one another. It was madness! Surely
they must feel like me, lost, confused, hurting,
anything but jovial. I'd wake up in a moment and I
really would be just an ordinary everyday teenager,
buying an apple or orange from that greengrocer.
But, no, I was in a cage with a group of no-hopers
who from all outward appearances considered it a
game and a comical one at that.

A screw (warder) unlocked the cage, my name
was called and he led me over to a section of the

reception area hidden behind a hospital-type screen. As well as several screws in uniform, one a medical officer, were two inmates. I was made to strip completely naked facing them as I took each item of clothing off. One of the inmates, who wore a red band of cloth around his right biceps indicating that he was a trustee, described each item of clothing in detail, then handed them to the other trustee who placed them in a box. 'They'll be washed and ironed at no expense in the prison laundry for you to wear at your next court appearance. Meanwhile, you'll wear prison uniform,' the trustee explained.

The medical officer approached me next. 'Turn around Halpin.' I did as requested. 'Now bend over and spread your legs, this won't take a second.' Complying with the order I gingerly bent over. I wanted to object to what was happening, but managed to suppress my outrage until he had completed his degrading inspection. Then I was given a bundle of bedding and clothing and allowed to shower and dress.

Next I was taken to a canteen area, given a meal and told to await cell allocation. Sitting at one of the unoccupied tables, I attempted to eat the sloppy looking excuse for a meal set before me and managed to get some of it down me, surmising this was what I had to get used to as far as the diet was concerned in this establishment.

Another inmate joined me at the table. ''Ow's it goin' mate, right stinkin' 'ole, i'n it, 'ey? What you in for then?' He looked at me for an answer. 'Err, I'm a house-breaker, you know, burglar,' I answered. 'That's aright then; as long as yer not one of those nonce cases.' (This was prison jargon for child molester.) 'Mind you, most of yer sex cases ask for rule 43 (segregation from other prisoners for protection) otherwise the other cons give 'em a good kicking, know that I mean? I'd be the first one in with the boot, I can tell you. What's yer name then, pal? I'm Joey Green from Canning Town, East Ender like, know what I mean?'

'My name's Paul, err, I'm not really sure where I came from. Probably Watford, Joey. Yeah, Watford's about right I suppose, although I feel more Irish than anything else.' Reluctantly I shared these things with him. Really, I wanted to tell him to sling his hook and mind his own business, but to get on the wrong side of this Cockney character would be a very big mistake. I didn't relish the idea of feeling the force of his GBH charges.

'Yer Mum and Dad Irish, then?' he asked.

'Yeah, Irish, that's what I meant, you know. I feel more Irish than English.' I wanted to get off this subject. The truth was I really didn't feel that my background mattered one bit at that moment, I didn't feel that I'd ever belonged or ever would to any particular group.

'Paddy's are aright, mate, nowt wrong with having green blood, loads of paddy's round the East End, I can tell yer, fightin' mad they are an' all, know what I mean? A' up, peter allocation!' Joey was referring to a screw who had come into the canteen. 'Quiet now, you lot, and listen for your names. As your name is called, pick up your bed bundles and form a line by the door.'

The officer began calling names from a clipboard that he held in front of him. Joey and myself were both called into line. Joey was behind me whispering in my ear, 'Looks like we might be lucky, share a peter together.' (A peter is prison jargon for a safe or a prison cell.)

We were marched along what seemed like miles of corridors, up several flights of stairs, until eventually we were brought to a halt on a landing with cells on either side of it. Joey and myself were indeed allocated a cell together. Our cell cards were placed on a hanging clipboard attached to the cell door. My card was red in colour, Joey's was white. The red card identified me as giving my religion as Roman Catholic, Joey's was white indicating he was Church of England. Printed on the card were name, number and date of birth, also date of admission into custody which was 23-11-70. I would be back in court before Christmas.

We were allowed a few minutes to fetch water from the recess, or slopping out area as it was known, then the cell door was slammed shut with no further ado.

There were bunk beds along one side of the cell. Joey quickly claimed the top bunk. Our toilet was a bucket. There was one table and two chairs, two metal washing bowls, a small prison-made brush and dustpan. Inside a pillow case included with the bed pack was one bar of crudely manufactured soap, a small tub of pink chalk-like toothpowder, toothbrush and an envelope with one sheet of prison writing paper for a letter which could be sent to relatives or friends free of change. We were not allowed to seal the envelope, as this and all other mail, incoming and outgoing, would be censored.

Seated at the table, I watched Joey get his bed made up. This way we would not get under each other's feet. Once he had finished his bed-making,

Joey climbed up onto his bunk and I also got my bed made up and lay down. I'd been in institutions before but never a real prison.

Joey talked non-stop and at great length about his criminal escapades. It was his third visit to Ashford and he had already been to Borstal. He was nineteen now and expected to go back to Borstal if he was found guilty of his present offences. He intended to plead 'not guilty' when he went for trial.

'Wanna smoke, Paul? I've got a bit of baccy 'ere,' Joey offered. I said yes, he handed me down the hand-rolled ciggy. Well, I couldn't get my hands on booze and in many ways that was a godsend, so I puffed away at the ciggy while I listened to Joey waffle on about life in the East End, about how he had a real cracker of a bird outside who would wait forever for him.

'When this is all over, Paul, I'm gonna pull off one real big job, a bank or jewellery hoist, set me and the bird up for life, know what I mean? Are you listening or what down there?'

'Oh, yeah, I'm listening, Joey. It's just that I've been doing a lot of heavy drinking recently. I'm still in a state of shock really, and to be quite honest mate, I'm not cut out for this prison lark. No, this is the last time for me, Joey. I'm gonna sort my life out, stop drinking and doing drugs, just live a normal life. This is a mug's game!' I finished.

'Well, mate, you know what they say, don't yer? If you can't do the time, don't do the crime. As for me, I can handle a bit of time. It gives me the chance to pick up a few tips, make a few contacts for when I get back out there. Na, mate, that so-called normal life would crack me up – no excitement in it. Still – 'orses for courses, like, know what I mean?'

The light in the cell went off. Joey informed me that the light switch was outside the cell and a screw would switch off at 10 pm every night and back on again at 6 am each morning. So it was now ten o'clock.

Joey passed me another ciggy. As he did so it suddenly dawned on me that I needed him. He knew the ropes around this place. I was going to need a friend to get by.

'Joey?' I called.

'Yeah, mate, what's up?' he replied.

'I think you're a sound bloke and I really hope you pull off a big one, then you can pack it in. Me, well, I haven't got what it takes.' I was attempting to flatter my cell mate.

'Well, thanks, pal. Tell you what, if you need a few quid anytime when you get out, pop up to Canning Town. I'm gonna be rolling in it, no problem. Stick around me while you're in 'ere as well, I'll show you the ropes, keep you out of trouble, like, know what I mean, mate. Let's get some shut eye now, eh? See yer in the morning, not that either of us is going very far in this place, anyway.' He finished with a chuckle at his own brand of prison humour. Then, at last, he was quiet.

The next moments I spent absorbing the prison sounds. Keys jangling, occasional shouts, even screams, then just the sound of my own sobbing. I cried myself to sleep.

Chapter 10

Promise Not To Laugh At Me

That first morning at Ashford Remand Centre was a nightmare in itself. Was I ever fortunate to have been placed alongside a cellmate like Joey! Without his cajoling and encouragement, I'd never have survived. When the cell door had opened that morning I'm quite sure I'd have stayed rooted to the concrete floor of the cell, such was the fear I felt as the prison came to life.

As I took my first steps out into the corridor, a water jug in each hand for hot and cold water for washing, I was caught up in a stampede of youths rushing in the same direction, and another similar stampede making their was back having completed the dreaded early morning slopping out routine. Prison officers stood to one side of it all as if cut off from what was actually going on around them. They showed little interest in the procedure.

Once inside the recess the stench was overwhelming and everybody was obviously in a hurry to get in and out as soon as possible. There was a lot of pushing and shoving, especially around the one outlet for hot water. Joey informed me that the supply of hot water ran out very quickly at slop out time.

I managed after a struggle to place my hot water jug beneath the tap, the water was still hot. Hot and cold water, one jug in each hand, I joined the flow of bodies back to the cells realising that my body was trembling. I must still be withdrawing from the booze, I thought, as finally I was back in the cell. That would have been no problem outside, a can or two under my belt – still the thinking drinker even in prison!

Joey had been on another errand. He'd collected the razors from the landing office. They were a specially adapted type: the blade could only be removed by a contraption kept safely in the office. 'I don't really reed a razor, Joey,' I told him.

'Yeah, I thought that mate, but seein' as you only gets one blade in a blue moon, and even then there's no certainty it'll do the job, I drew both for this cell and will use one then the other, get my drift?'

'Yep, that makes sense, mate,' I replied.

The door was opened again twenty minutes later to enable the water to be disposed of. Joey agreed that he would do this, if I went to the library which was in fact a cell with some prison-constructed shelving and a few rows of books. I found the cell which doubled as a library. Never really being a reader, I picked several books at random for myself, and several tatty, much-thumbed crime-type novels that Joey had requested. 'To see if I can pick up any good ideas, for future reference, like,' he had said. One shelf I noticed had a sign attached to it. 'Chaplain's selection', and on it were several Bibles, copies of the book of common prayer and other religious sorts of stuff. Taking one of the

Bibles I sandwiched it between two other volumes I had chosen. If people thought I was reading the Bible, they'd think I was a right wimp, especially in prison. Then there was Joey – what would he think, bringing a Bible into the cell?

Joey was back in the cell, sitting at the table, smoking. He offered me a ciggy which I took.

'All done in here?' an officer's voice came from behind me as I sat at the table with Joey. I'd placed the pile of books in front of me, then the door slammed shut once again.

'What we got 'ere then, mate?' Joey had found the Bible. 'Gonna get religion, while yer 'ere then, or what?' he said sarcastically, but not too unkindly.

'No, not really. It just happened to be there, so I thought "Why not?" Might bring me luck when I go back to court if I read a bit of it.' Making this reply seemed somehow about the truth. I couldn't think of any other reason for bringing it into the cell.

'Well mate, read away, but don't start preaching to me. I'll stick to this.' He held up one of the paper backs. *True Life Crime Stories*, the front cover announced.

The cell door opened again. 'Breakfast, lads,' the screw at the door almost shouted.

Meals were taken in a huge hall. This and exercise time were the only times the whole prison population come together. Breakfast consisted of porridge (which I later discovered was top grade pig meal), an ugly looking prison-made sausage, which was mostly fat-soaked bread crumbs, bread and margarine, and a mug of tea (commonly referred to as diesel) without sugar.

This dining hall was the noisiest place I'd ever been in. Inmates shouted across the tables at one another, sometimes making loud threats and curses. Joey sat opposite me, occasionally engaging in conversation with the West Indian youth sitting alongside him. They seemed to know each other. The lad next to me had asked me typical prison questions – 'What are you in for?' 'When do you go back to court?' 'What sentence are you expecting?' etc. Joey interrupted, 'Like a zoo in 'ere, 'n it, Paul?' he addressed me.

'Yeah, it is a bit noisy,' I replied.

Then we were filing out of the hall, back to our cells. Back in the cell Joey climbed on to his bunk with his crime book. I decided to scribble a few lines to my Dad. Maybe he'd be sober enough to make some sense of all this. Signing off, 'your ever loving son, Paul', I felt a pang of longing to be just that, 'a loving son'.

The rest of that day was spent seeing different members of the reception board which consisted of the governor, chaplain, doctor and a probation officer, each of whom said they would compile a report on me which would help the court come to a decision about sentence. I wasn't allowed to know at that stage what recommendation they would make. This, for me, was a punishment in itself. The uncertainty of it all gnawed at my mind constantly.

After lunch, which I did eat even though it looked like it had just been scooped from a trough in a pig sty, we had an hour's exercise. Joey had said that it was important to get your system used to prison food, after all, there wasn't much else on offer just now.

I saw several inmates I knew from outside and one lad from my approved school days. Harry Pearce was a lean six-footer with red hair. In the approved school he had been known as a bully. He strutted around the yard with an ape-like individual who I would certainly have avoided down an alley on a winter's night, or any night come to think of it.

Finding myself alongside Harry and the ape, I reminded Harry of approved school days. The way the ape looked at me when I'd approached them made me feel I'd made a big mistake, but nonetheless Harry spoke, or rather bragged about how he'd been the Daddy of the school and had more or less run the whole show. I remembered how he had bullied smaller timid lads into homosexual acts with him, myself included. I wondered how his hardman image would stand up if I were to spread that around the prison.

'Yer know what, Sam,' he spoke to the ape. 'I kept all the smokes and extra grub in that place, even had a wimp to clean my shoes and make my bed' (and sleep in it with you, I thought). 'Life of luxury it was. Ask 'im, 'e'll tell yer – Butlins 'oliday Camp, weren't it mate? Tell Danny 'ere.'

'Oh yeah, real holiday it was, err, real holiday.'

Joey was just a few yards ahead, mumbling an excuse to leave. I caught up with my cell mate. He introduced me to the lad with him.

'This is Mouse, Paul, lives two roads away from me on the out. Real name's Alec, but he's got ears like a mouse.' I looked at Alec. He looked very mouse-like, not just his ears but the general shape of his whole head, even down to the attempt he was obviously making to grow a moustache; the growth on his upper lip was more whisker than moustache.

Mouse and I exchanged greetings, when I said 'hello' I thought he might actually 'squeak' his reply. His voice was very high pitched. He'd certainly been labelled with the correct nickname but his 'hello' back was entirely human. People with nicknames, I thought, are either instantly likeable or on the other hand, quite detestable. Alec, or Mouse, was the former. Mouse was sharing a story with us about his Dad who was a rag and bone merchant, or a 'totter' as they were known around London. His Dad, he told us proudly, was one of the few totters that still travelled the streets with horse and cart collecting scrap iron which they sold on to scrap metal dealers. His Dad no longer bothered with rags as there was no money in it. Mouse was awaiting sentence at the Quarter Sessions (now known as Crown Courts) for a string of shop break-ins and assault on the police. He'd already been to Borstal twice and at twenty years old would probably receive a couple of years YP (Young Prisoner). He'd more or less resigned himself to that fate.

Round and round we shuffled the circle of the prison yard, the sixteen-foot-high fence topped with razor-sharp barbed wire, discouraging any attempt to escape. We were not allowed to halt at any time. All conversation had to be carried out on the move. After an hour we were led back to our cells. At four o'clock, back down for tea. After the meal a final unlocking for fresh water and slop out, then bang up (lock up) for the night. This was to be the routine every day; it rarely – if ever – changed, Joey told me.

Joey was engrossed in the paperback. Laying underneath him in the bottom bunk I thumbed through the pages of one of the volumes I'd taken from the library, a novel by someone called 'Daphne du Maurier'. I tried reading the first chapter, finding myself reading a paragraph again and again because I kept forgetting what I'd read; my mind was too caught up with the dilemma of this place and the forthcoming court case.

I picked up the Bible, toying with the idea that maybe this so-called Holy Book might provide a way out or relief from the anxiety and fear that I was feeling. Finding the book of Isaiah, chapter thirty-eight, I read from verse seventeen,

> *'Surely it was for my benefit that I suffered such anguish. In your love you kept me from the pit of destruction; you have put all my sins behind your back.'*

Having no knowledge of the Bible, these words surprised me because certainly, in a crazy sort of way, the anguish I was feeling was beneficial. Drink had been really giving me a hammering. At the moment it was unobtainable. Therefore, at least physically, time in prison kept me from my own personal pit of destruction. And I supposed it was God that Isaiah was talking about having *'put all his sins behind his back'*. I'd made a full confession about the break-ins, and intended to plead guilty in court, so surely God had put that lot behind his back as well. Now God needed to have a word in the Judge's ear to somehow get me off with a light sentence.

At the front of the Bible was printed a list of where to look when faced with certain sets of circumstances, giving Psalm 34 as a reference to look at. Let's give that a shot, then, God. What are you going to tell me next? Well I had to admit this mental exercise was taking me beyond the circumstances I was in. It would be a bonus, of course, if Jesus or an Angel would sort of suddenly appear and just let me have it from the horse's mouth, then we would all know where we stood, then I wouldn't need this Bible. Looking up the Psalms, I looked for and found number 34.

Reading slowly through the verses, I came to verse 4 which says,

> 'I prayed to the Lord, and he answered me; he freed me from all my fears.'

I carried on reading verse 5,

> 'The oppressed (yeah, I suppose I was oppressed) look to him and are glad; they will never be disappointed.'

Looking around the cell, I was still convinced that only myself and Joey were present and that didn't make me feel very glad and certainly I still felt disappointed about being in gaol. On to the next verse, the sixth,

> 'The helpless call to him and he answers; he saves them from all their troubles.'

Now that little bit sounds good.

'What's up, mate? Did yer say something? What sounds good?' Joey quizzed me. I must have spoken out loud.

'Oh, nothing, Joey. I've been trying to work this

Bible stuff out – got a bit carried away, that's all, no problem,' I said.

'You wanna watch it, Paul, I'll tell yer, it starts just gettin' you curious, then it gets a grip on yer, like. Saw a thing about it once on telly. All these black folk jumpin' around like right nutters, and one of 'em, I think he was the actual vicar, wrapped a load of snakes round his bonce and really started ranting and raving about Jesus. Don't try and suss that stuff out. Take my advice, it'll send you loopy just like them black geezers. Know what I mean? Ere you go mate, have a fag, take your mind off all that God stuff.' He passed down a ciggy. I lay smoking the ciggy, contemplating what I'd just read in the Bible, also what Joey had said about religion driving people loopy. Surely those words I'd read had some meaning for me. If I'm honest with myself something other than fear had taken place somewhere inside, almost as if just the effort of searching the Bible for help had been rewarded with some sort of peace from a fairly hopeless situation.

I whispered some words to God saying that I was sorry for everything and could he help me to understand just who he was. I was still full of doubt, yet things had already happened in my life which couldn't be just explained away as coincidence.

'Joey, are you asleep?' I asked.

'Nah, mate. Can't sleep with that light on. Why, what's up?'

'Promise me you won't take the mickey if I tell you something that happened to me once when I was a kid, because it really did happen,' I said.

'Go on then, let's hear it, anything to pass time

away. And I won't take the mickey, promise yer,' he answered.

'When I was a kid, I lived in a convent for a while. Things had happened at home that weren't too good. My Mum and Dad were fighting one night, a neighbour called the police and me and my brothers and sisters were just grabbed, put in a minibus and taken away. Anyway, that's how I came to end up in this convent.'

'Now, Joey, this next bit is what you promised not to laugh at, and you did promise for real, didn't you?' There was a pause as I awaited his response.

'Swear on me Mum's life, good enough for yer?' he said quite solemnly. 'Now get on with it.'

'One day I had this tremendous pain in my jaw. One of my teeth at the back, a molar, had become infected. I'd never felt so much pain, it was agony, worse than being in here even.'

'Cor blimey, that must have been pretty bad then.'

'Well, anyhow. In the convent you had to go to church a lot, almost every day, but there was no choice. Well, you see, sometimes I served on the altar, helped the priest like. You know, an altar boy.'

'Yeah, I know the sort of thing, dressing up in frocks and that, and bowing to one another, what a load of old cobblers. I feel sorry for you mate, I really do.' He prompted me to go on.

I continued, 'Well when I was having all this pain, I went to one of the nuns. Balling my eyes out, I was, and I begged her to get me to a dentist. It was a holiday period, she said, and I would have to wait a couple of days. She gave me a couple of junior asprin and told me to be brave.

'She sounds like a right cow, that one. I'd have sorted her out, good and proper, I tell yer. Anyway, what's all this toothache and stuff got to do with church and being an altar boy? Yer losing me, mate. Get to the nitty gritty of it.' He was getting impatient.

'Well, the priest once told me that Jesus could perform miracles today, just like he did a couple of thousand years ago. So I remembered this and I locked myself in the toilet with this pain and I asked him to take the pain away, Jesus that is. And as sure as you and me are in this cell now, that pain went there and then, honest it's the truth, so surely there must be some truth in what the priest told me. What do you think?' Joey didn't answer straight away, when he did, his reply surprised me.

'I suppose you could have been healed. Whether it was this Jesus you're on about, couldn't tell yer. Yer see I only believe what I can see and touch. It's a nice story like but it just sounds a bit too far-fetched for me. Maybe it was a coincidence and the pain would've gone away on its own.' As he was talking, the light went off. 'Get some kip, Paul. Nice story, though, must admit, nice story.'

'Thanks for not laughing, Joey. Couldn't have handled that right now.' I meant this as I said it.

'Toothache's not funny, mate, miracles or no miracles, Jesus or no Jesus. Just don't go loopy on me while yer 'ere, there's enough nutters around as it is, know what I mean?' He turned a few times above me, then the cell was silent.

I lay listening to distant sounds. There was a motorway close by and traffic hummed along in the night. How I longed to be a passenger in one of those vehicles taking me anywhere. A lump formed in my throat. Crying, I asked once again for Jesus to do a miracle, just as he must have done years ago in that convent. Please God, show me it wasn't a coincidence, prove it to me. I fell asleep.

Chapter 11

Christmas In Prison

The day of my court appearance finally arrived. A prison officer unlocked our cell early that morning and gave me just ten minutes to wash and pack my prison kit. Secretly I nursed a hope that I would be back on the street that day. Saying goodbye to Joey, I wished him luck when his trial eventually came up.

In the reception area I was given my own clothing back. Putting them on again increased the hope I was feeling that it would be all over today. They'd just put me on probation or something, or maybe a fine. Anything other than more time in prison cells.

Another uncomfortable ride across London to Watford in the inhuman box of the Black Maria.

Once in the cells beneath the courthouse, fear crept in again, my stomach turning somersaults. A key turned in the cell door and the duty solicitor was shown in by the gaoler. The door closed behind us. He shook my hand and introduced himself as Mr Proctor. 'We chatted briefly when you were last here, if you remember, Paul. The court has now allocated me to your case officially. Obviously you need to agree to that. If you agree I need your signature on these papers.' He handed me several typed documents. Not bothering to read them, I signed each one. All I wanted was to get out of here as quickly as possible. If this bloke could help make that happen, I'd sign anything.

'What's going to happen today, then, Mr Proctor? Just give it to me straight, I want to know.' Yes, put me out of my misery, I thought. It seemed like a lifetime before his reply came.

'Well, Paul. I've seen a copy of all the reports that have been compiled and the general opinion, in particular the prison doctor's opinion, is that you need help as much as punishment. His report shows great concern regarding your consumption of alcohol. He has, if fact, diagnosed alcohol addiction.' He went on, 'The general recommendation is that you receive Borstal training.' Stopping now that he had given it to me straight, he waited for a response. All I was thinking about right now was where was my miracle? What a let-down God was. Where was Jesus in all this Borstal talk? What this bloke was telling me meant I would remain locked up.

'OK, Mr Proctor, you've told me now. Thanks for not beating about the bush.' He looked relieved that I'd taken it this way although I, myself, wasn't sure how I'd taken anything. I'd been mercifully struck numb. Hopefully it would be a permanent numbness.

The solicitor had gone now, all that was left was the waiting, always waiting. Then the gaoler came and took me to hear my fate.

Standing in the dock now, I listened to the

Magistrate remand me in custody with a recommendation that I go to Borstal. It was not in this court's power to pass that sentence. I was to be sentenced at next Quarter Sessions, a date to be fixed.

Back at the remand centre, I was allowed to rejoin Joey in the same cell.

'Tough luck, mate. Told you that religion stuff wouldn't help, didn't I? Yer might as well get used to the idea, you're goin' to be off the streets for a while.' He sounded almost pleased about it.

'Suppose you're right, Joey. All over, bar the shouting,' was all I could say.

'How long will I wait now for sentence?' I asked Joey.

'Three to six weeks, usually. Your area don't 'ave such a work load as London does. Yeah, about a month, no more, you'll be all right mate. Hang on in there.' Joey's answers were always fairly accurate, he knew a lot about the system and how it worked, probably more than the so-called professionals. I was lucky to have Joey around.

Christmas arrived. I'd never been excited about Christmas, so I certainly wouldn't be this year in a cell, waiting to be sent to Borstal. My Mum and Dad both sent cards with money. At least they did that! Christmas time in Ashford was a time when some of the restrictions were lifted, and they allowed money to be spent in the prison shop. I treated myself to a small radio, proper soap, toothpaste, etc., also sweets, cakes and fruit and several ounces of tobacco. The prison food was also changed; it was actually quite edible, and there was plenty of it. The governor and all his staff (well, most of his staff), for Christmas day at least, treated us all as humans. That evening a service was held in the main chapel for those who felt led to attend. I went, leaving Joey in the cell. Surprisingly the chapel was quite full, though most just saw it as an opportunity to get out of the cells for a while. A Salvation Army band had been invited in. As they played and sang traditional carols, some of the prisoners and staff joined with them. While other prisoners cat-called and heckled, the band played on regardless. The screws turned a blind eye to it all, even when some of the inmates began to shout obscenities at the females in the band. At the close of the service, the Governor and a Captain of the Salvation Army each gave a Christmas message, then the Captain ended the evening with a prayer for both staff and prisoners. Then we were led back to our cells. The officer who ushered me into the cell lingered long enough to say, 'Happy Christmas'. I looked at him and returned the greeting. Our eyes locked just for a second. His eyes said, 'I'm just a bloke doing my job, it's not my fault.' I wonder what he saw in mine that Christmas night?

'We've got a special treat tonight, Paul.' We were sitting at the table facing each other. Joey was teaching me some card games. 'Yeah, a very special treat.' He said this tempting me to ask what this treat was. I'll play along with him, I thought. 'A treat, 'eh, Joey? Don't tell me Santa is actually coming to the cell? Problem is there's no chimney for him to come down,' there was just a little sarcasm in my voice.

'Nah, mate, this is our treat.' His hand went inside the waist of his trousers and he withdrew it with something clasped in his fist. He opened his hand and a black lump fell onto the table. Hashish.

'Well, mate, wanna get stoned for Christmas? This is what you call a miracle, yer know what I mean? Ha, ha, ha!'

In no time he had made a joint, lit it, and almost forced it between my lips. I puffed away on it, at the same time nervously eyeing the cell door, expecting a screw to burst in and catch me. Joey saw my nervousness. 'Don't worry about the door. Look,' he pointed to the gap at the base of the door where a wedge had been lodged. 'You just enjoy that dope, ain't no screw coming through there, I can tell yer, just trust me,' he rolled another joint. I was down to the roach on the first one. I was already buzzing. Joey took the stub from me and tossed it through the cell window. The second joint was passed back and forth across the table. Joey had a Cheshire Cat type grin across his face. 'How's it hittin' yer, mate? Good stuff, eh! Put that little music box of yours on.' He was referring to my radio.

The transistor radio was under my pillow. Rising from the table to reach my bunk, my head began to spin. I fell onto the bed, boy, was I stoned. 'Err, Joey, could you, err, deal with the radio, I'm sort of, err, you know?' I couldn't finish what I was trying to say. 'Stoned, mate, that's what you are. Stoned.' He reached over for the radio, fiddled with the controls until he found what he wanted, then clambered up onto his bunk.

The joint came back down to me. Taking several more large lungfuls, back it went to Joey.

Closing my eyes, I was aware of the radio playing and the slight rocking of the bed as Joey beat his mattress in time to the music that was playing. At one stage I was aware that Joey was shaking some perfumed talc around the cell, especially around the door area. I must have nodded off as I hadn't heard him climb down from the bunk. Joey saw I was awake. 'Had a little snooze, then? As you can see, I'm just trying to get rid of some of the smell, the screw'll be doing lights out in a minute. Don't wanna rub it in, like, do we? The wedge can come out now, as well. Security don't allow keys on landings after ten. So we can smoke without fear of the door bursting in.' As he spoke the Judas hole slid across. The screw doing the final count of bodies was humming some Christmas ditty to himself, the light went out, the screw was gone.

We now sat again at the table. Joey lit a candle. 'Where on earth did that come from?' Now I was impressed.

'Somebody nicked it from the chapel. Gave him a couple of ciggies for it.' We lit up a joint each, this time. I just took it easy. I didn't want to make a twit of myself, throwing up or something.

'A drink wouldn't 'arf go down well with this 'ere dope, wouldn't it, Paul?' He smacked his lips as he said this.

Strangely enough, I hadn't given booze much thought since my arrest. 'Problem with me, Joey, if I had one drink now I'd want more and more. One drink's too many, a hundred's not enough.'

I don't know why – probably the dope – but Joey found this statement hilarious and roared with laughter. His giggles were infectious and soon the two of us were creased up laughing. In the next couple of hours we smoked joint after joint. Finally we both fell into a drug induced sleep on our bunks, waking only when the light came on at six in the morning. I still felt stoned. Shaking the talc around the cell as Joey had done the night before I prepared

111

for the cell door opening at seven. Satisfied there was no sign of drugs in the cell, I waited for the familiar rattle of the key in the door. Christmas was over, it was just another day beginning in prison. This was reality for me at the moment. For a few hours my mind had been freed with the unreality of dope, but the heavy cell door and four walls reminded me of where I was really at. Survival meant acceptance. I was beginning to realise this. The cell door opened and the prison came to life.

On Boxing Day, the prison routine was more or less back to normal. The meals that day consisted mostly of Christmas left-overs which was still a big improvement on the usual menu.

That evening a film was shown in the prison gymnasium. I thought it strange that the choice of film should be a gangster movie. So much for the rehabilitation! It was obvious to me that prisons like this were nothing more than schools for advanced crime education. No doubt many of the young criminals would be re-enacting scenes of the movie in their already damaged minds, some probably in time to come acting those scenes out in real life. Myself – I was also fantasising throughout the film, especially during the robbery scenes. It stimulated the criminal side of my character. Everybody wanted to be a somebody, didn't they? Why not a successful criminal? After all, I now had a record that would follow me everywhere. The label had already been stuck to me. If I wanted to get a proper job, I would have to lie about my past and even if I lied my way into work when I was eventually released, the past always would catch up with me: someone would always point the finger.

Back in the cell that evening, again I began to flip

through the Bible. Joey was playing some solo card game at the table. This seemed to keep him locked in concentration. I was glad about this as conversation of any kind was the last thing I needed at that moment. Why the need to go back to the Bible? Surely it had already let me down? A glutton for punishment, me. Same with the drinking outside – going back to the things that let me down.

Everything seemed to be going from bad to worse. This was another situation the Bible said you could find help for in Scripture. Hebrews 13 was recommended:

> 'Remember to welcome strangers in your homes. There were some who did that and welcomed angels without knowing it.'

God was a comedian as well, it seemed! The next verse completely wound me up.

> 'Remember those who are in prison as though you were in prison with them.'

Well, God, I can hardly forget any of that, now can I? Look God, can't you see I'm at least giving this a try? I'm searching for some meaning to my existence which until now hasn't been much of anything at all. And seeing that you know everything anyway, you already know this, so how about some help while you're at it? Oh, forget it – it's obvious you've written me off as a hopeless case. Look at yesterday: Christ's birthday. Even here in gaol I got stoned. If drink had been available I'd have got stuck into that as well. Yeah, you're right – I'm hopeless! Let's forget it!

Closing the Bible I began to toy with the idea of speaking with a vicar or priest while I was in there. Crickey, was I feeling desperate! After lights out, I tried praying again in a whisper so as not to disturb Joey. The more I prayed, the angrier I got with God. Eventually I prayed for sleep. God – if indeed it was God – at least granted me that release from my surroundings. I slept.

After slop out next morning, I went to the landing office and made an application to speak with a member of the clergy. After lunch I was taken to the Chaplain's office. Although I was registered as a Roman Catholic, the Chaplain on duty was a Church of England vicar. I said I had no objection to speaking with him.

The vicar asked me about my circumstances, why I was in prison, etc. Was I a Christian? Answering 'No' to this seemed true. I didn't really understand what it meant to be a Christian and told the vicar briefly that I had prayed at times but wasn't sure that it was getting me very far. I did tell him about the convent and the healing of my toothache, so I did believe in something.

'Paul, one thing you can't have is God on your terms. In fact, it's exactly the opposite. God, if you are serious with him, wants you to accept him on his terms. When you eventually are released, are you determined that the drinking is going to stop? From what you've told me, if you continue drinking on release you'll be paying many visits to us and other places like this. I believe that's what you need to be sure about. God gave us all free will – the choice will always be yours. The story of Jesus dying on the cross for sinners, which means **all** of us, can remain just a story. On the other hand, his death and his resurrection can be applied to all on a personal level and that starts with repentance, truly from your heart, not just being sorry for what we've done, but turning away from the things that lead us astray. In your case certainly the booze and drugs need to go completely.'

He'd finished talking now. It was obvious it would always come back to the demon drink. God's way or my way? It seemed so easy but something of the rebel in me still rose to the surface. Given the right circumstances, I could and would get my drinking under control (that lie again).

'Well, thanks, Vicar. I'll think about what you've said and, err, if you could, err, would you say a little prayer for me now and again? Maybe God will listen to you.'

He nodded and smiled meaning he would, then called the officer waiting outside. I was taken back to my cell.

Chapter 12

Wormwood Scrubs

On the seventeenth of January 1971 at Herts
Quarter Sessions I was sentenced to between six
months and two years of Borstal training. Until the
Judge actually pronounced sentence, I nursed the
hope that somehow my luck might change. Alas,
what the prison recommended was put into force.
When the Sessions ended that day, myself and
half a dozen other prisoners were loaded into the
now familiar Black Maria and transported to
Wormwood Scrubs Prison in West London.
Although this was an adult prison, it was also an
allocation centre for Borstal Trainees. The Scrubs
housed some of Britain's most dangerous thugs. It
was also one of the most secure institutions of its
kind. Prisoners under eighteen years of age were
known as baby burglars.

The reception routine was identical to that of
Ashford. Unlike Ashford, however, baby burglars
did not share cells. I was taken to 'B' wing and
locked up on my own. In the cell I found a list of
rules on the one table provided. Reading through it
I began to wish I was back at Ashford. No laying

on beds during the day, cell floor to be scrubbed everyday, a bucket and scrubbing brush was provided for this job. The small army type bed was to be turned on its side and leant against the wall by 9 am and not to be put down again until 4.30 pm. This deterred sleeping on the bed during the day. As this was winter, jackets were to be worn at all times when inmates were not in cells. This included the slopping out periods.

The light switch was inside the cell, at least I could choose when to be in darkness or not. With my bed made up, I stretched out upon it and stared up at the ceiling. No Joey to amuse or annoy me. I would have given anything at this moment to have him sleeping above me, waffling away in his Cockney accent. Lying there, feeling quite sorry for myself, something attracted my attention; a voice.

'Oi, mate! You in cell twenty-four. Come to your pipe.'

'Pipe? What pipe! Crikey! There's somebody under my bed,' I spoke aloud to myself.

'Are you deaf in there! Come to your pipe!' The voice again. Louder this time.

Getting to my feet quite startled I cocked my ear in the direction I thought the voice had come from.

'Can you hear me? Follow the heating pipe to the wall on the left-hand side, where your bed should be.' Then silence.

At the back of the cell, several feet below the heavily barred window, a cast iron pipe ran, apparently through both sides of the cell walls. My pillow end of the bed almost touched the pipe where it disappeared into the wall, facing the window that would be on the left side. I pulled the bed away from the pipe and waited.

'Have you found it yet?' The voice came from a gap in the brickwork, surrounding the ancient heating system.

Lying there on my bed, face down, my head was just an inch or so away from where the voice had come from, although it seemed to have come from beneath my bed.

'Hello there. Yes, I've found it.' I waited for a response.

'Got you at last. What's your name, mate? Mine's Larry.'

'My name's Paul, Larry. Just got sentenced today. Pleased to meet you.' Meet who? I hadn't met anyone. I was talking to a voice coming out of a wall. I felt a proper idiot.

'Now, look here, Paul. Listen carefully. If you ever feel like a chat during the lock up, just give two raps on the pipe and that'll get me to the talk hole. Also, we can pass items through the hole to one another. You know, ciggies, matches, that sort of thing.' As he spoke, a sheet of paper, a newspaper appeared my side of the hole. Pulling it through I unfolded it (it was, in fact, two pages folded over several times) and several hand made ciggies dropped out.

'Thanks, Larry. Give us a rap if you need a fag yourself. I bought a couple of ounces through with me, so I'm not short. I've got matches and ciggy papers as well.'

He told me how lucky I was to have got tobacco through. It was usual for the screws to confiscate any amount over half an ounce. Then it was usually shared out among the trustees working reception duties.

'You must have had a good shift of screws down

118

there, tonight, mate! Your luck must be in. Anyway, I'll let you settle in for the night. See you at slop-out in the morning.' Then he was gone.

Sleep eluded me. Although physically and emotionally exhausted I couldn't shut off. I lay in darkness, somewhere someone sang, another screamed abuse from a cell window at an officer walking in the grounds below. 'Get down from that window, you rat-bag!' the officer shouted back. I was curious to look from my cell window now, so I got out of my bed, and standing on my chair, looked out onto the prison below. This part of the prison was four floors up and I found myself look- ing out across Scrubs common in one direction and prison buildings in another. Floodlights lit these buildings up which gave them an almost ghost-like aura.

It was quite cold standing there, so I moved back to my bed, got beneath the covers and hoped for sleep. Cursing several times out loud at no one or anything in particular, I began to wish I was dead. Cursing again and again, then crying. In one instant, the Judas Hole moved across and a night light came on operated by the screw outside. I uttered another curse, not loud enough to be heard through the door. An eye was just visible at the Judas Hole. Hatred for the person who owned that eye filled me. There was something obscene about being scrutinised though a small hole in a door, so even more obscene must be the character who chose to make it his job. I smoked one ciggy after another, at the same time going through a thought process of killing at least twenty individuals who I felt were to blame for the mess my life was in, includ- ing my Mother and Father and people who had emotionally and sexually abused me in children's homes I'd lived in. Most of all I blamed God for allowing things to happen. I hatched plots to kill and maim individuals when released. Oh, how people would suffer for what they had done to me! They would pay one day, yes they would all pay, and pay dearly.

My head began to ache. 'Oh, God, why the torment? Just let me go to sleep and never wake up again. What was there to wake up for?' I cried aloud. Moments later, regretting the murderous thoughts, trying another form of release, I cried out for forgiveness to that same God I felt had caused all this. I repeated the Lord's prayer over and over again, out loud, not really believing it would do any good, but just the sound of my own voice was better than the awful prison silence. I still had my radio. I tried listening to that for a while, turning the tuner from station to station. Listening to the words of a song now and then, all the words seemed deliberately aimed at winding me up. The temptation to smash the ridiculous little machine to pieces was so strong that I switched it off and shoved it under my pillow before I actually did just that.

This was, it seemed, the longest night of my life. Time just went on in slow motion. Occasionally I went to the cell window and stared out into the night. A bat flickered past my window. 'Even you, you ugly little thing, have got it made compared to me' I whispered at the night sky where the bat had appeared.

Back in bed again, tossing and turning, I tried to shake off the thoughts that flooded through my mind.

At some point my brain must have just switched

off and with that eventually came sleep. When I opened my eyes again, it was daylight. The prison was coming to life, keys jangling, raised voices, names being called out, bedlam itself. My first day at The Scrubs was about to start. I had to survive. The need to be one step ahead of the system was important, nobody could or would see anything like defeat in Paul Halpin. I arose to meet the challenge of Wormwood Scrubs. The cell door opened. 'Slop out, and scrub out.' The screw's voice addressed me, then was gone on to the next cell.

Following the train of bodies along the landing I completed the slopping out process. There was a bit more order in here than at Ashford, not so much pushing and shoving. Having collected hot and cold water I made a second journey and filled the scrubbing bucket.

Someone stood by my cell, an inmate. 'Hi, I'm Larry. We spoke through the pipe last night. Sleep all right?'

'Oh yeah. Like a log.' I lied, moving into the cell. Larry followed.

'You can get away with just wiping the floor every other day, scrub one day, wipe the next.' He indicated the bucket of water I'd placed on the floor. 'Well, I'll leave you to it. The screw will be locking up again now, anyway.' He made as to go, hesitated and said, 'Get your bed up, against the wall for nine o'clock. They do an inspection then. Some screws go by the board, others, well, you know, easy going. But first morning and all that, it'll pay to get it right. Tell you what, we've got a minute. Come next door and I'll show you how it's done.'

I went to Larry's cell. He'd already had some time at it by the look of his layout. Taking it all in I thanked him and went back to cell twenty-four, my cell. The landing officer soon came and banged the door shut behind me. Remembering the layout of Larry's cell as well as I could, I set to work. Bed against the wall first, bedding hung over the framework. That looked about right. Looking at the floor, then at the bucket, I was thinking 'Scrub or wipe? Scrub. Yes, scrub. I remembered Larry's advice, 'first morning and all that,' so I scrubbed.

Satisfied with my efforts, I realised that these early morning tasks might be painstaking, but they left me feeling a physical relief if nothing else, that first morning.

Now I sat at the table, rolled a fag and waited. 'Yes, I will face the day, there's no choice,' I whispered to myself. My cell door opened. 'Breakfast!' the screw barked. 'And don't forget to take bowls and mugs down with you, for that lovely porridge and your early morning pint of diesel.'

Amongst my kit I'd found a small plastic pudding bowl and pint mug, also plastic. Taking these with me I headed for my first breakfast at Wormwood Scrubs.

Chapter 13

Keeping an Open Mind

After breakfast at about nine o'clock we slopped out again. All meals were eaten in cells and my food was luke-warm by the time I'd collected it from the hot plate area on the ground floor. Cold porridge and bacon didn't appeal to me that first morning, but I ate the toast and margarine. The remainder went to the swill bin, where it probably came from in the first place.

The routine cell inspection took place. Two officers carried this out in almost complete silence, just an occasional grunt of what could have been approval or disapproval, who knows? As they were leaving the cell, one screw who wore a crown on either shoulder of his uniform jacket said, 'You'll be taken through what is known as induction, this morning, Halpin. An officer will collect you when they are ready for you. OK, lad?'

'Yeah, OK,' I answered.

'And by the way, laddy,' he was shouting now; one minute nice as pie, now hollering at me. What did I say or do wrong? 'When you address myself or any other officer in this establishment, it's "Sir" or

"Yes Officer". Do you get my drift, you horrible little criminal?' Finished, he glared at me, waiting for a response.

'Yes, Sir, I get your drift, Officer.' My reply came with as much sarcasm as I thought I could get away with.

'Watch this little low life, Officer Glover, maybe he'd like a few days in the block (punishment cells).' He addressed the screw who accompanied him. Then he slammed the cell door shut and was gone.

All of a sudden I was tired, so tired. The bed beckoned me, no chance even of just laying down for awhile. Sitting at the table I lay my head on my arms and just waited. Waiting was what it boiled down to, that was prison in a nut-shell. A waiting game.

A while later, I was collected for induction. This was a real farce. Myself and a group of others were introduced to the various heads of department, the head tutor of the education department, the clergy, medical staff, a psychiatrist included. To round the morning off, we were taken to the prison shop and library. In the shop we were given a small amount of tobacco, cigarette papers and matches. Non-smokers could choose sweets instead, or soap, toothpaste, etc. All, if not nearly all took smokes; it was apparent that most inmates were smokers.

Back in my cell at lunch time I thought about the morning induction and the people we'd been introduced to. The truth was they saw groups of inmates like us on a daily basis, it was all just routine for the staff. When they looked at one inmate, he was no different than the next. Just another carcass to be processed through the

124

system. If you wanted to be an individual in prison you somehow had to stand out. That would be difficult as most of the time was spent alone in your cell.

In the library that morning I'd selected some reading material. One book was a true life story. It was the author's own experience; he'd been a criminal who had found God and changed his life around. The introduction stated how he was now a reformed character and was working as a social worker in London. He was also a lay preacher. A right do-gooder by the sound of it, but deep down as I read this book, or parts of it, I envied the bloke's changed life.

There was an hour's exercise at 1.30 pm. In the yard I teamed up with Larry, my next door neighbour. He gave me a rough idea what to expect during my stay on 'B' wing.

'By the way, Paul, that loud mouth who screamed at you this morning. Don't take it on board, he's just a frustrated Sergeant Major, not man enough for the real forces. So he takes it out on unfortunates like ourselves. He always picks on newcomers. Tomorrow it'll be someone else. Just keep your cool, yes Sir, no Sir sort of thing and you'll get a cushy allocation out of here. OK?'

'I'm grateful for that, Larry, because deep down I thought I'd gotten off to a bad start. Thanks a lot.' And I was relieved, I'd been secretly nursing an idea that I was to expect a lot of stick from that bloke, the screw who had inspected my cell.

'Have you already been allocated then, Larry?' I asked.

'Yeah, mate. Portland I'm going to. Got violence

on my record. You got anything violent like?' he asked me.

'No, I'm just a thief really who likes getting drunk. Got caught in someone's house, and, well, here I am.'

Larry told me as we walked around the yard that people like me usually went to borstals classed as being open establishments. He also told me that if you were considered a druggy or an alchy there was a place called Feltham in Middlesex which housed all sorts of nutters and was more like a hospital than a nick.

'From what I gather, if you're not mad when you go in, you are when you come out. Mind you, you're never the same after any of this prison lark,' he added.

Listening to Larry was important. From my time spent with Joey in Ashford, I knew that survival meant very often listening and remembering what you heard. You just had to get wise enough to be able to separate the lies from the truth.

'When will you go to Portland then, Larry?' I asked.

'Who knows? Maybe a few weeks or more. Depends on the length of the waiting list' he replied.

We began filing back into the wing. Before we were banged up, Larry took me to his cell and gave me several old newspapers, the most recent of these was two days old.

'When you read what's going on out there, mate, it doesn't seem quite so bad in here. I'll tell you, the real criminals are out there, we're just small fry.'

Back in my cell, I glanced through the newspapers. Everybody, according to the Press, seemed to be at it one way or other. My cell door was opened and I was ushered out by an officer. 'You're to see the chaplain, Halpin. Come with me!' he said.

The officer escorted me to the chaplain's office which was situated in another part of the prison. On the way we went through a wing which was abnormally still and quiet.

Chancing a conversation with the screw, I asked him what wing this was.

' "A" wing, this is, laddy. I dare say you'll be giving us the benefit of your company here one day. The men on this wing are long-termers, serving anything from five years to life. A few will even die here. The end of the road, you might say.' He didn't say this unkindly, just matter-of-factly.

'No, Sir. I'm making this my first and last visit.' This I said quite convincingly.

My escort laughed at this statement. 'I'd be a rich man if I had a pound for every one of you inmates that had said that. I could take early retirement on the proceeds, I can tell you.'

We arrived at the chaplain's office. The screw rapped on the door. It was opened by a priest and I was shown in. The officer left me with the priest.

'Sit yourself down, young man. Let me see now.' He leafed through some papers on his desk. I sat in a chair opposite him.

'Ah, here we are. Halpin. Paul Halpin.' He looked up to me from the file he had been referring to for confirmation that it was Paul Halpin seated there.

'Yes, that's right. Err, do I call you Sir, or what?' I wanted to get this right from the start.

'Not at all, lad. You call me Father John. That'll

do nicely.' He was smiling at me now. Then, 'Are you a practising Catholic normally, you know, when you're a free man outside?'

'No, not really. I was in a Catholic convent as a child. I suppose then I was but, no, I don't go to mass any more if that's what you mean, Father, or any other church either.'

'OK, and yes that's more or less what I wanted to know.' He wrote something down on a piece of paper in front of him.

'One of my jobs as clergy here, Paul, is assisting the system in placing you in the right training Borstal, so I'll be submitting a report with some suggestions to the allocation board, OK?'

'Yes, father. I understand.'

'How have you coped so far? I see here from your file that you were in Ashford for a while and arrived here just a day or so ago?' He waited for my answer.

'I'm getting used to it, Father' I said. This was true, all you could do was get used to it, otherwise you would crack up.

'Would you be interested in the services here? There's a mass on Sundays and if you were interested we have a group that meets on Wednesdays for a Bible study and discussion.' He asked if I should be included for both of these. I said I'd like to. It would be time out of my cell. There was no religious or spiritual motive behind my answer. He asked me about my stay in the children's home, how I came to be there. He listened as I told him about my father's alcoholism and the fighting and arguing in the family home. He ummed and arred and occasionally tutted when I shared a particularly nasty bit. I shared also that my drinking habit had also got out of control prior to my arrest.

'Yes, your case notes say you're alcoholic. Do you agree with that completely?'

'Well, Father, as I said, drink played a big part in life. If I hadn't been so caught up in booze I wouldn't be here; I'm quite sure of that.' Having told the priest this, I wondered if I might be setting myself up for Feltham, the nutter's place. Too late now, I'd done it.

He asked me more about my background, more or less the same things they had asked me at Ashford.

'Well, Paul, nothing else we need to talk about just now. I'll include you on the church list for Sunday and also Bible group on Wednesday. The Bible study is a joint venture with C of E and Catholics getting together. Occasionally we get a guest speaker or two from outside. Makes it a little more interesting.' With that he summoned 'B' wing by phone and the same officer arrived seconds later and escorted me back to my cell. The evening meal was being served when we arrived back.

Just after the bang-up that evening, Father John came to my cell and gave me a Bible.

'I meant to give you this during the interview. It can be good company at times like this. Try reading it, even if just a little at a time.' He said goodnight and left me on my own again.

My bed was down now, so I lay on it thinking about the day's events. It was a great relief to stretch out and in a way I actually welcomed the solitude of the cell. It was obvious to me now that in order to be free sooner rather than later, I would have to toe the line, show a willingness to change, even if that meant a bit of grovelling to the powers that be. There would be people I liked and people I didn't, also those who would like me and those who wouldn't. Somehow, a balance had to be found.

The Bible the priest had left me was on the table. I got up off my bed, went to the table and picked it up. Weighing it in my right hand I said out loud, 'Show me you're real, then. Or is this just another book? Let's get straight with each other!'

I lay back on my bed and thumbed through the pages of the Bible. Someone had written something in the back of the Bible, various verses. Galatians 6 caught my eye, and by it was a page number, nothing else. I searched for the page number written down. It was in the New Testament. Reading from the start of chapter six, I browsed through the verses. Verse seven leapt out at me with an almost physical force.

> *'Do not deceive yourselves; **no-one makes a fool of God. A person will reap exactly what he sows.'***

Immediately I felt conviction – I'd uttered those words just moments before! 'Show me you're real then, or is this just another book?' echoed through my mind. Why had that priest just decided to bring me a Bible? He could have done that in the morning. Why was I drawn to the writing at the back of the book? It's that priest. He's got psychic powers or something. I turned to the back of the Bible once more. 'There's got to be a good bit for me in this somewhere, surely. Anyway, was I reaping what I'd sown? I'd done a few jobs, now I was in jail, don't tell me the big man upstairs was going to get on my case as well?' There was reference to a book called

Hebrews. The writer (I'm sure it was the priest) had put in a suggestion to look at chapter twelve, verses five and six. Again I found this in the New Testament. 'Well, if nothing else I'm getting to find out the different books of the Bible, and that's not a mockery, God, if you are there somewhere,' I said aloud.

Reading from verse five the words hit me between the eyes again.

> 'And you have forgotten that word of encouragement that calls you sons: "My son, do not make light of the Lord's discipline, and do not lose heart when he rebukes you, because the Lord disciplines those he loves and he punishes everyone he accepts at a son."'

Closing the Bible, I considered, not mockingly, but with an open mind what I'd just read. Certainly it seemed more than just a coincidence that, yes, in many ways my life had been a mockery of God, and if that last part I'd read was true, and it did seem to apply very much to my present situation. The way I saw it was this. God was sorting me out, not because he took pleasure in it, but because he loved me. If it were true, then all was not lost. Picking up the Bible again, I just held it tightly in both hands and said out loud, 'An open mind. Even if I have serious doubts about this book, no more mocking, just an open mind.' I switched my light off, went back to my bed, and crawled beneath the covers.

Drifting in and out of sleep, I found myself reliving the experience I'd had as a child, the one that I had shared with Joey – when I'd asked Jesus to heal my painful mouth and the pain had gone immediately. Coincidence, fluke or just luck, or an act of God, a miracle? Why not a miracle, Paul? A voice was whispering, why not a miracle? My own voice whispering, or God's?

Chapter 14

Facing Painful Memories

The first days at Wormwood Scrubs were difficult, to say the least. Getting used to the idea of not being able to lay on my bed during the day, the ludicrous task of scrubbing the floor every morning, eating alone in my cell. I began to long for my eventual transfer to training borstal, yet I'd only had a few of the many induction interviews, and until these were all completed, the allocation board couldn't even consider a move to another establishment.

When I was eventually taken from my cell for an interview with a prison psychiatrist I'd become quite depressed, not just with my surroundings but with life itself. It all seemed so pointless. I'd started mentally craving booze and I'm quite sure had anything containing alcohol or some other mind-altering chemical been available I'd have taken it regardless of the consequences.

In the hospital wing, the interview with the shrink took place.

'Good morning, Paul. I'm Doctor Miller. Sit down, will you?' He indicated a chair and I sat down.

He got up from behind his desk and from an adjoining room he'd gone to, he came back pushing a mobile desk which he wheeled over to where I was sitting.

'On the desk in front of you, Paul, you'll see several boxes. Open box 'A'. It's clearly marked as are the others. Have you opened it? Ah, good. I see you have. Now complete the puzzle you see in the box when I say go. Understand?'

I nodded that, yes, it was understood. Looking up for confirmation to go ahead, I saw that the shrink now had a silver coloured stop watch in his right hand.

'Ready, steady, go.' He gave the command to commence. The puzzle consisted of pieces of ply wood cut into various shapes, matching holes for each shape had been formed in the bottom of the box, rather like a jigsaw.

What a carry on! To add to the embarrassment I already felt, this crazy shrink had come to stand behind me so he could look over my shoulder at my efforts. I wanted to just burst into hysterics. What could this kids stuff possibly have to do with serving time? The pieces hadn't all found a home in their corresponding holes when the doctor called time. He almost snatched the box from the desk so I couldn't attempt another correct placement. What a wally! This bloke was a fruitcake, not me. The urge to laugh welled up again. Surely this idiot wasn't serious about all this. He sat opposite me at his desk, he was scanning first the incomplete puzzle, then me, then he would scribble away at a notepad in front of him.

There followed a similar process with three other puzzles. One of these consisted of three figures without arms or legs, an ape, a man and what appeared to be a bear dressed in a clown's costume. The idea was to match the limbs, which were loose in the box, with the figures. I just couldn't take it seriously! I stuck the arms and limbs willy nilly, none of the figures got the correct limbs, arms went where legs should have been and vice-versa. When he'd stopped me on this puzzle, I was actually expecting some adverse reaction from him, but no, he had just looked first at the puzzle, then at me, and carried on with his scribbling.

'Would you like a cigarette, Paul?,' he offered.

'Yes I would, Doctor. Thanks very much.' I was about to get up from my seat to receive the cigarette from the packet he was holding when he flicked the packet at me. It landed in my lap. The packet contained just one fag. I searched for my matches.

'No smoking in here, lad. Disgusting habit. Try and give it up while you're in prison.' Then he went back to his scribbling. 'You just gave me the fag, you raving idiot' was what I really wanted to say, but instead, 'I'll try after this last one, Doctor,' is what came out of my mouth.

'Are you a homosexual, Paul?' He had finished his scribbling. He looked directly at me now as he asked this question.

'No, I'm not a queer, Doctor, if that's what you mean.'

'If you like to use that term, queer, then yes, that is what I mean. Bearing in mind that you are yourself in a queer situation, are you not? (implying queer) Do normal lads of your age break into other people's homes? Or drink or take drugs in order to face life? I think not. Then it depends what you define as being queer lad, doesn't it?'

'Well, yes, I err ... suppose it does really.'
'Careful now, Paul' I was thinking as I answered. Something told me there was a method in this shrink's madness.

'I'm gonna ask you to share some things with me, Paul. Only if you want, though.' He paused as he opened a drawer to take out some paperwork.

'Ah, yes. This is it. These papers contain some pretty disturbing facts compiled by various groups of people and individuals, policemen, social workers, members of staff from various children's homes you were housed in, etc, etc.'

'You see, Paul, according to these reports, not only are you a culprit, but you have also been a victim. the fact that you have committed crimes cannot be condoned, certainly not by me. But very often certain events in your childhood, in anybody's childhood, even mine, can explain certain behavioural patterns later on in life.

'Does that make any sense?' He was trying to draw something from me, I began to feel uncomfortable. This man had suddenly become exactly the opposite of the twit I'd taken him for earlier. This was now the professional at work.

'Yeah, I suppose if things had been different, with my family and that, you know, more settled like normal families, it could have worked out for me. Who knows? Maybe I wouldn't have ended up in a mess.'

'When you were very young and went to the convent, St Joseph's, some men that befriended you there, members of staff, took advantage of you. Do you want to tell me about it?'

'I don't know, really. Don't see the point of it. I

didn't realise anybody had written it all down.' I fidgeted in the chair.

The Doctor continued, 'Yes, not just those incidents, but others as well. Now, in your own words, try telling me about it. Again, Paul, you don't have to. It's your own choice. By the way, if you've got a match, you may have that ciggy now. That's not in return for anything, either. Let's just say, as an ex-smoker, I can appreciate the need at a time like this.' I lit up and at some stage I began reliving some experiences from the past.

I'd not been at the convent very long and already I'd run away twice, only to be found several miles away, wandering through the streets. I was taken back to the convent. As I was handed back to the nuns, the sister superior cooed to the WPC and male policeman about how I would be loved and cherished. It was the second time I'd scarpered. When the police had gone I was dragged by my hair into a study. One of the nuns pulled my shorts and pants down as I was forced to bend over a desk. My buttocks were then beaten repeatedly. I was filled with so much fear during this beating that my bowels opened. For this I was dragged into the communal bath house, thrown into a cold bath and repeatedly screamed at and told that I was a filthy little devil. At this time I'd have been about five years old.

There were several male workers at this home. From what I can recall they seemed to be people with time to spare. They volunteered to teach things like woodwork. Some took us for games; table tennis, snooker, etc. One evening I went to the woodwork class. The teacher there was quite funny, he just said and did things that were funny. I was

drawn to him and tried to please him by being help-
ful, fetching wood and tools and he seemed to like
me as well. One day I went to the toilet which was
situated in a shed like building adjoining the workshop. I went into one of the cubicles, finished in the
toilet and came out. The teacher was there, smoking
a cigarette.

I made to walk past him to get back to the workshop. As I did so, he put his hand on my shoulder.
He offered me the ciggy. Taking it from his fingers,
I puffed on the fag. Some of the smoke went down
my throat and made me cough. 'Didn't think much
of that, sir,' I said and gave him back the ciggy. It
had made me feel sick. Then quite unexpectedly he
clasped my chin, tilted my head back, stooped down
and kissed me on my lips. He had a full beard, it felt
horrible, unnatural.

'Don't tell anyone. You could get into trouble,'
he had said after the kiss, leaving me unsure
whether he meant the smoking or the kiss. Well, he
was an adult, a grown man. I knew something was
wrong, but surely a man kissing a boy was wrong?
Still I'd keep it a secret: the thought of another
beating like the last one didn't bear thinking about.
Kissing a man wasn't as bad as a beating, after all.
It wasn't very nice but maybe it meant he liked me
more than the other kids.

One day he asked me to stay after class to help
him do some cleaning up for him. 'You're more
reliable than the others,' he'd said. That made me
feel good. Sort of special. So I said I would. When
everybody else had gone, I swept the workshop
floor and tidied the tool rack. He showed me how
to oil the planes and vices in the tool cupboard.

When we'd finished we had a cup of coffee from

the flask he always brought with him. We didn't ever have coffee in the convent, so this was a real treat for me. I'd forgotten the kiss, or rather pushed the incident to the back of my mind.

Somehow I ended up sitting on his lap, and this didn't feel right to me either. I made to get away from him. 'Sister Veronica will be wondering where I've got to, can I go now?' He held me closer and tighter as I said this. Wriggling to get free just made him hold me even tighter.

'Don't rush off now, you're safe with me, the nuns know that.' His beard was pushing against my mouth. His breath smelled of tobacco. 'Look, this is bad, surely we're not allowed to do this?' It wasn't me doing anything! But suddenly it was we, not him. I was part of it.

'Just keep still for a while, then you can go. I'll not tell anyone what we've done, don't worry. It's our secret, I promise.'

He was an adult, far stronger than me, but at last with a mighty roar I wrenched myself from his grip. At this moment something in my five year-old being died. I was in hysterics, he was as well for different reasons. He was pulling my clothes back on which he'd removed earlier. 'Come on, Paul, stop that noise! You'll bring the nuns running in here, then we'll both be for it, won't we, eh?'

Then he talked me into what he saw as the right way of seeing things. I grew up for a moment, thinking, do what he wants, agree with him, he's as frightened as you are. Eventually I got away from him, but only after he had warned me that he was a respected member of the Catholic Church, and that it was a real live Bishop that had given him the job at the Home and if I told anyone about what had happened, they wouldn't believe me, just punish me for making up stories.

'Just let me out of here. I'm not going to tell anybody, I promise. Please open the door and let me go!'

Dr Miller brought me back to the present. 'Once you start, you can't stop, can you Paul? But it would be wiser to stop now. It's a painful experience that's always been there, that's obvious, and in the long run it's that kind of deep hurt that causes resentment and in your case, distrust and who could possible blame you for that? This may all sound very complicated psychiatric jargon to you, but, you see, just now and again I come across a case like yours that's genuine. In my job I interview and test many inmates every year, most are liars, some live in a real fantasy world, real for them anyway.

'I'm sure that many inmates have had experiences like yours that never came to light. Others, and I've met them, who won't get the help, even when it's discovered sometimes years later that they've been victims also. We've run out of time.' He looked at his watch. 'Paul, you're probably going to feel quite vulnerable over the next couple of days. What people have described in the past as feeling exposed. If it gets too much for you, report sick to your landing officer at slop-out. You don't have to give a reason. Then when you are taken to the medical officer, tell him you want to see me, OK?'

The officer came to take me back to my cell. I'd been with the shrink for three hours.

That night was spent in a great deal of confusion. Not only did I feel vulnerable as the Doctor had said I might, but I was feeling anger like never before towards that man at the Convent. After all that time I wanted to see him punished for what he'd done and then there was the realisation that there had been other men like that afterwards. Did I really want to share any more of my past with this doctor? Why should I even trust him? He was, after all, a complete stranger. No enough was enough. There was, however, a kind of relief, from somewhere deep within, something had dislodged itself and come out, in relating all that horrible experience to a complete stranger. I was quite sure had anyone else tried to get that lot out, I'd have refused. It was strange, but somehow I felt a certain amount of trust towards this Dr Miller and I couldn't remember feeling trust towards any other human being. It was trust that had died within me years ago in that workshop. That so-called respectable Catholic teacher had murdered part of my childhood with his assault on me and had killed my trust. Maybe this was a time for rebirth? But certainly I would tread with caution. After all, you can't really trust anybody these days, can you?

Chapter 15

A Missed Opportunity

A week had passed since I'd seen Dr Miller. In that week, an education officer, a social worker, another member of the clergy and a representative of the allocation board (who was also an officer who worked on the wing) all saw me.

The education officer was a female teacher and quite an attractive one at that. Her job was to assess inmates as to what standard of education we would have, if any. She achieved this by a standard exam especially prepared by the home office for borstal trainees. About fifteen of us were tested together in a portacabin building somewhere in the grounds of the prison. It was the first room I'd been in without bars at the windows; on Sunday I'd gone to the chapel and even that was not completely without barred windows.

The officer who had been our escort to the portacabin had stationed himself outside the entrance. I wondered, however, if the teacher felt safe with fifteen or more growing youths, who spent the best part of any given twenty-four hour period alone in a cell where the only relationship with a female would be in the imagination. But apart from the odd lust-ful stare and from one braver inmate, a lewd comment regarding her bust, the session in the education department went off without incident. So, it seemed, my induction period was complete, the wait would begin now for an allocation board to sit and decide to which establishment I was to go.

Wednesday evening. My cell door was unlocked by Mr Lockyear, who it turned out was one of the more humane screws. He didn't seem to believe it was below an officer to pass the time of day with an inmate.

'Your name's written down here for Bible study, young man. Feel like going? Break the night up for you, lad.' He had a sing-song sort of voice.

'Yes, Mr Lockyear. Anything to get out of this cell for a while,' I said.

'Make your way down then, lad. Ground floor, there's a few other inmates waiting. I'll meet you down there. I've got two more lads to collect up here. Meanwhile, I'll bang your door shut. Rumour has it that this place is full of thieves.' He gave a chuckle as he shared his attempt at light-hearted humour with me.

There were one or two jokes that Larry had been telling me through the pipes at night about prison officers. I was sorely tempted to chance telling Mr Lockyear one of them. Thinking twice about it, I headed towards the staircase which would take me to the ground floor.

The Bible study was held in the Church of England chapel. About forty people attended, forty inmates that is, plus the Catholic priest, a Church of England vicar and two civilian lay-preachers.

143

There were twenty adult prisoners and us baby burglars. The first time, apart from when church services were held on Sunday, that I'd ever been so close to inmates from the adult side of the gaol.

'Now then, chaps. Let me introduce you to our guests tonight. We have tonight Mrs Jane Carson and Mr Ted Barnes.' The vicar who was doing the introduction indicated the two civilians. Then he went on. 'They are both members of churches outside in civvy street and feel that they have been called by God to preach the gospel of Jesus Christ within the prison system.'

'Nothing but do-gooders,' the lad next to me whispered. 'Mind you, she's a bit of alright, that Jane tart. She could spend a night in my cell anytime.' Then he was craning his neck forward, I presume to get a better look at the female visitor. I was no prude, and yes, she was a good looking female. Already I was beginning to resent this bloke. All I wanted was the chance for this time out of my cell. Lucky enough he'd now turned his attention to the inmate sat the other side of him. The woman was now standing and the vicar was saying she had prepared a little treat for us. She had a guitar and was now tuning it in while adjusting the microphone which had been placed in front of her. She spoke into it, 'Evening guys. Nice to be with you tonight.' There was a pause. She scanned her silent audience. Was she looking for a response? If she was it didn't come. 'Well, I hoped it would be nice to be with you tonight, that is.' She exaggerated a look of rejection as she said this.

If she was looking to win her audience over, her ploy seemed to have worked. The response was laughter and applause and a few wolf whistles thrown in. The ice was broken.

She sang and played very well, a sort of folk type style of music, about Jesus and his love for the sinner and outcast. At one stage she got her audience to clap and sing along with her. I was beginning to feel really glad I'd come, it was pleasant to listen to this woman with the soft-singing voice.

When she had finished she handed over to the male visitor. He gave a testimony about how he had become a Christian. He had been a bit of a rebel himself. 'The only difference in our situations is that you broke the unwritten eleventh commandment, that is, thou shalt not get caught.' Laughter from the audience, including the four screws among us. I wondered just how much they identified with the unwritten commandment.

We all were asked to join in the Lord's Prayer towards the end of the evening. The Catholic priest then closed with something called a benediction.

'Now before you leave and the officers take you back to your cells, Jane, would you like to say something?' The priest then invited her back to the microphone.

'Well, gentlemen. We trust that this night has in some way blessed you as much as it has myself.' She paused and cleared her throat, then continued. 'What I'd like to do, and I'm sure God would like it as well, is to invite you into the Kingdom of God. Now, that may sound weird to some of you, maybe all of you.' She paused again and took a deep breath and went on. 'God loves you all so much, even though you've blown it and ended up here. Jesus was no ordinary man, who could perform

145

tricks for money or any other gain. Jesus identifies with you, not your sin. He was without sin, he knows rejection, he was also rejected. He knows what it is to be an outcast: he was an outcast, and if you don't take anything else back to your cell tonight, picture the crucifixion if you can. To be crucified was in Jesus' time the punishment of criminals. Jesus was crucified between two villains, just like you and me are villains in different ways. But Jesus, the Son of God, who hadn't done anything wrong, was innocent of any crime, yet he didn't cry out, "not guilty, your honour," but cried out, "Father, forgive them for they don't know what they are doing." We, that is, everyone in here, are the ones who deserve the cross. Not God's son, but us. But it was love that took Jesus to the cross, God's love for the whole of his creation. And God wants none of you to be lost, he's calling you tonight, to repentance and salvation. Who is going to respond to that call? We're running out of time so I'll not beat around the bush. Who wants to inherit eternal life, tonight? Just stand where you are now as a sign, not to me but to God himself, that you are willing to accept Jesus into your life and repent of the past.'

She went back to her seat. The church had become completely silent. I chanced a look around the church, most of the audience had their heads bowed. The screws were looking a little flustered in their seats. It would seem we had gone well over our time this evening.

The chap in the seat next to me got to his feet. Crikey! He was crying. Now there's one for the books. Earlier on he was calling the speakers 'do-gooders' and the woman 'a tart'. The tears were

146

real enough, though. Either that or he was a good actor. There were ripples of laughter among the rest of the inmates, and some embarrassed coughs and grunts coming from the screws who must have been keen to get us back to our cells by now.

The two visitors brought the evening to an end with a final prayer of thanksgiving for the one soul who had stood up, apparently he had received salvation, whatever that meant. Secretly I admired him, crying in front of everybody, as well, must have taken a lot of guts.

Back in my cell later that night, I pondered over what I'd just witnessed. Maybe I had missed out on something important. I actually envied the bloke who had stood up and cried. Hadn't he, after all, been the exception that night? I hadn't stood up, mainly, because I was concerned about what other people might think. In prison surely you followed the pack? That was easier, you didn't get any hassle that way, did you? 'Oh, I don't know, must get some sleep anyway,' I said out loud to myself.

Before I got into my bed, I gave Larry a bang on the pipe.

'What's up, mate? What do you want?' he called through to me.

'Larry, have you ever been to one of the Bible talks, like the one I went to tonight?' I asked him.

'No, why would I want to go there? I don't believe in all that God and Bible stuff.' He sounded peeved with the whole question I'd asked him. It was obviously not his favourite subject.

'Larry, do you know what salvation means, like, if you looked it up in a dictionary? What does it actually mean?' I cocked my ear, awaiting his reply.

'Well, it might have something to do with Sally

Anne (Salvation Army). I dunno, mate. To be quite honest, I couldn't give a monkeys either. Good night, mate.'

Switching my light off first, I got under my covers. 'Yeah, who gives a monkeys?' Soon I slept.

Chapter 16

Reliving Sexual Abuse

The next day was Thursday and I was taken to see Dr Miller again.

Feeling quite nervous this time and also quite embarrassed, I took the seat he once again offered as I was shown into his office. I felt quite different this time. This man had been allowed an insight into my past, not just some report he had read, but from my very own mouth. Did he think now that I was the one to blame, at the time of the assault, or at least afterwards? I felt that it was my fault, it was me that was guilty. That somehow I'd allowed it to happen.

'Do you still feel guilty, Paul?' He's read my mind, I thought as he said this.

'Guilty? Guilty about what, Doctor?' I pleaded ignorance.

'About the past, about this man and what he had done. Most victims do, you know, blame themselves in some twisted way. But let me assure you. You were, and are, not guilty of anything at all. You were vulnerable, a child. Completely innocent of any wrong.' It certainly sounded like he was on

149

my side. He went on by asking me to say out loud that, 'I am not in any way to blame for what this man has done, he was a perverted and sick man. and I did not deserve that to have happened.' I did as he asked and repeated what he told me.

Then he asked me how the man was found out, eventually. Going back in time, I began to relate just what had happened.

Some time after the assault, I had a conversation with one of the other boys at the home, John. We were talking about this and that, as children do. We were in the refectory area of the home where we ate our meals. We were talking about the staff, those we liked and those we didn't like so much. The man who had assaulted me was mentioned.

He was the only person that we both agreed we hated, not just disliked but hated.

'Why do you hate him so much, then, Paul?' John had asked. 'Come on, you tell me first,' he coaxed, though we both knew why.

Coming clean first, the words just came out. 'Because he's dirty, he's a dirty man. He does bad things to me and if anyone finds out, I'll get a hiding, that's for sure. I'm a kid and he's an adult. They'd believe him, wouldn't they? He's done it to you as well, hasn't he, John? Come on, you're my friend. Hasn't he? He's done bad things to you as well? We won't tell on each other. Come on, tell me.'

He did. John told me that almost an identical assault had taken place against him in the work-shop. The only difference was he had committed rape on John, and had hurt him and made him bleed. Afterwards the man had sneaked John to the showers and washed the blood away and made John change his pants. He gave John a monopoly set for being so brave.

We were trying to decide what to do. Should we tell someone? No, we'd get walloped. Then, maybe run away and tell the police what happened. At that moment, the decision was taken from us. The kitchen door behind us opened and both John and I spun around. Sister Bernadette stood in the doorway. She'd listened to every word. I waited, we both did, expecting a hiding. It never came. 'Go to your rooms, both of you. You're not to tell a word of this to anyone. Leave it to me, you understand?' 'She must believe us,' I was thinking. It sounded as though she was on our side.

'Sister, we're not liars. Not about this thing, anyway. We swear to God that we're not. Isn't that right, John? Tell sister what I've said is true.'

'It's all true, sister,' is all he said.

'Of course I believe you, boys. Now run along, say no more, not another word.'

Our assailant was never seen again by either of us. He just seemed to vanish. Weeks later the sister superior summoned me to her office and told me that things had changed at home and would I like to live with my Dad for a while to see if it might be better for me? I said yes. Without further ado she, herself, packed a small case for me. I wasn't allowed to say goodbye to anyone. Several of my brothers and sisters were also in the home somewhere. It seemed they were staying, I was going. I was in Watford a couple of hours later.

Back in the land of the living now, the doctor asked me if I'd felt glad that the man had been found out.

'I don't remember what I felt, really, Doctor. One

151

moment I was in a children's home, next thing I knew, my father was back in my life, but that didn't last long anyway. I arrived home to find my Dad had a girlfriend living with him, and her children. We'd been in a home and my Dad had moved another family in our place. The woman and her children, all three of them, treated me like a stranger. Soon I began running away from home and playing truant. One of my brothers and sisters joined me back at my Dad's later on, but soon all three of us were whisked back to the convent while this woman and her children stayed in the family home. You can imagine we were really mixed up now.' The doctor listened to my acount of things. I decided to tell him more.

'When I was about twelve, they sent me back to my Dad's again. He was drinking heavily most days and nights and in between worked as a labourer for sub-contractors on building jobs. The same atmosphere had once again prevailed in the house. More drunken rows with this woman, just like with Mum, and now two lots of children were in the middle of it all which made it even worse.

Then something happened to me and I ended up in another children's home. Come to think of it, that was the last real contact as a child I had with my Dad, or my Mum, in a family sense that is.'

'Yes, the something that happened, as you put it, is all down on record. I have a documented account of it here. Tell me about it if you can. I want to help you, Paul. You've survived some very hair-raising stuff and you've impressed me. Somehow, I see a strength in you that one day may be really beneficial in your life. Now tell me what happened in your own words and how you went back into care.'

For a moment I pondered over what he was asking me. I had some smokes already rolled in a tin. Taking it from my pocket, I raised it as an indication I wanted to smoke. He just nodded his consent. I lit up.

It was some time in the 1960s, that's as close as I can get to the year. I'd be about twelve years old, maybe thirteen; I'm not really sure. I was staying at my Dad's in this strange set-up with this other family. Some of my real brothers, and a sister, were also around. And I believe that the others were either in Institutions or with my Mum. I would go to my Mum's house a few miles away sometimes, and I can remember some members of my family being around at that time.

A school was found for me nearby but I rarely attended. No-one really seemed to bother to check up on me. I'd made a friend in the area called David who was about the same age as me. We went on shoplifting sprees together. We played truant, spending these times in some woods we'd discovered were a good hideout. We both had bikes which we had nicked from the local baths. We kept these hidden in the woods when we didn't ride them, taking them to the road when we went off on a spree of petty theft. They were our get-away vehicles as we saw it then.

One day we stole some sausages and eggs and from a hardware shop, and a frying pan to cook them in. We made a small fire in the woods before we realised we needed cooking fat. David set off on his bike to get some. By the time he got back I had a really good fire going. Once the food was cooked, we ate off two tin plates with forks that David had brought back. Along with the lard he'd also nicked some soft bread rolls. I really liked David: he was my only real friend. When David wasn't around, I preferred to stay alone.

We were disturbed that day by an older boy. He was suddenly there asking what we were doing. He had a snooty accent.

David, being bigger and braver than I, asked him, 'What's your game, creeping up on us like that? Been spying on us, I bet. Why don't you clear off, mind your own business! Get it?'

The last two words were said as a threat to the intruder.

'Look, lads...' The intruder sounded quite hurt by the reception David had given him. He explained his presence in our camp. 'Sometimes I take a short cut through here – I live nearby. I smelt your fry-up and saw smoke. I was just being nosey, if you like. Sorry! I'll push off.' He made to leave.

David called him back. 'Look, whatever your name is, it's OK. Just don't creep up, all right? What is your name, anyway?'

'My name's Reginald' he replied.

'Ooh, ahh, say!' David mimicked his posh accent. Then he said, 'I'm not calling you that! What's your nickname or something?'

'Reg will do, if you like. But Reginald is a nice enough name, though people do tend to call me Reg – except Mummy and Daddy – they never shorten my name, of course,' he finished.

'Mummy and Daddy!' David mimicked. 'How old are you? Fifteen, at least, I'd say.' David looked at me and asked, 'How old do you reckon Reg is?'

'Oh yeah, fifteen I reckon. Older than us, anyway. But then there's two of us, isn't there, Dave?' We couldn't have this bloke think that his age bothered us, I thought.

He seemed all right. A bit posh and that, but he seemed to accept us. Maybe we should do the same.

'Are you fifteen, Reg, like we guessed?' I asked him, trying to sound friendly.

'Fifteen yesterday, actually. Good guess, both of you!'

'There's a couple of bangers left in the pan. You can have them with the last roll if you like,' David said sounding a bit friendlier.

'Look, you two, I really didn't mean to intrude.' He said this as he helped himself to the last of the food.

'You seem a game pair. I've met this man, a nice sort of chap, lives in Watford. I've not been to school today. Played truant. Spent the day at his place. At a guess, you're doing the same – am I right? Playing truant, that is? He's got a lot of money and lots of food around the place. He's got a telly as well. We could spend the day at his place. He won't tell anyone about playing hooky either. He's decent like that. What about it then?' He seemed really keen to get us involved.

'Where could we meet you tomorrow, if we said "Yes?"' Dave asked.

'Meet me at Watford Junction Station. It's only a couple of minutes from his place. What about it then – is it a deal pals?' He really sounded eager.

We looked at each other, my friend and I. 'It's up to you, Dave. I'll go if you go,' I said.

After asking a few more questions, Dave said we would meet him. We made him promise to keep

155

quiet about our bikes being hidden in the woods. He wasn't stupid, this lad. He could see that neither we nor our families were likely to have afforded to pay for such good machines.

The lad, Reg, left us to go home. We had arranged to meet at three o'clock the following afternoon at Watford Junction.

When I arrived home, Joan (that was the woman my dad was living with) clumped me around the head with a shoe. 'Your own father doesn't know what you're up to, but I do.' With that she gave me another wallop, this time with her hand. I ran out of the house. That was it. They could keep my dad and the house. I'd never go back there! They were all no good. I was better off on my own.

That night I slept in an all-night launderette – well, not really slept, but at least it was warm. And nobody was around to lash out at me. My dad was just as much to blame for all this. He'd traded me in for this other family. As far as I was concerned I had no family.

I called on David the next day. It was about 8.30 in the morning. His mother thought we were going to school. Instead we went to the woods, collected our bikes and rode them into town. Telling David about what happened the night before didn't worry me; David was my friend. When I told him I'd been out all night he got a bit concerned about the police. 'They might be looking for you,' he said. As far as I was concerned, nobody would be that bothered. I convinced him it would be all right. I'd just keep out of the way for a while.

At three o'clock, after hiding our bikes, we met up with Reg. He took us to an address about a mile away. He shared with us a plan he had to steal money from this man if he got the chance and we could do the same if we wanted. ' After all, he's got plenty, I'm sure, so keep your eyes open for a chance.'

We reached a house that had been converted into flats. Reg rang a door bell. A man answered the door. He was a short, squat individual with really curly hair.

He said 'Hello' to Reg, then looking at myself then David, exclaimed with a grin, 'You've brought a couple of mates along then. Come on up boys and shut that door behind you. Can't be too careful these days, can you? My name's Bill,' he told us once we were in his flat. 'Most folk around here call me Curly on account of this lot!' He ruffled his hair and laughed. He looked at us, first David, then myself, then Reg. 'Well, I'm waiting – what do I call them?'

'Oh, I'm sorry, Bill – this is Paul and his friend David.' He indicated which was which. Bill offered me his hand to shake in greeting. I took it. His hand felt oily and sweaty and something about that handshake wasn't quite right. I had a sudden flash of the past. A workshop in a children's home ... no, couldn't be. Besides, there were others here anyway. This bloke Reg would have known. Surely, if he was one of them, he would have told us?

The flat was really just a bedsit; a large room with cooking facilities, two beds, a couple of armchairs. Bill and Reg sat in the armchairs, David and myself sat on one of the two single beds.

'Been to school today then, lads? Or bunking off like I used to? Oh, don't worry if you've been play-ing hooky. Your secret's safe with me. Ask Reg here, safe as houses I am, aren't I, Reg?' He looked at Reg for confirmation of this.

'Yes, you can trust Bill,' he said enthusiastically.

'Want some entertainment? I play the banjo, you know.'

He produced a banjo and began strumming a tune on it. He was really quite good. Perhaps I'd been wrong; he was really just a lonely sort, who enjoyed a bit of company.

He made us some tea and handed out plates of biscuits and cakes. I was quite hungry and they went down well. Bill could also do card tricks. He showed us a few. He was very good!

I needed the loo. 'Err, Bill, where's the toilet? I need to go.'

He pointed to the door. 'On the anding, first door on the left. I'm the only one on this floor, so I've got it to myself,' he said. I found the toilet. Instinct told me while out of the room to get away from here. I should've reacted to that instinct but back I went to join the others again.

We had been there for about an hour when Reg said he had to leave. 'Before I go, Bill, could I have that money you promised me for that little favour.' Suddenly Reg looked and sounded a little anxious. Dave spoke next, 'Why are you going? Wait for a while and we'll all go together.'

'No, I've got some jobs to do at home. I've sort of promised my parents. Can't let them down, you know.' He looked at Bill. 'About the money, Bill? Then I need to go. But if you like I'll come back later.'

The man withdrew a wallet from his back pocket, took several notes and handed them to Reg. As he did so he said, 'Don't forget our little agreement now, will you, Reg?' Then they went to the door and hushed words were exchanged briefly as Reg left. Then there were just the three of us.

Bill sat back down. 'He's a bit of a scallywag, is Reg. A bit light-fingered. Have to keep an eye on him.' He got to his feet again. 'Got some things to show you, up there.' He pointed to a trap door in the ceiling. Give us a hand with this, will you?' he said meaning a table which was pushed in one corner. The three of us manoeuvered it until it was directly under the trap door. This done, Bill stood on the table, pushed the trap door open and partly disappeared into the loft. He conveyed several boxes from the loft to the table and replaced the trap door, having moved the boxes onto one of the single beds. He then employed us again to move the table back to its original position in the room. Dave looked at me and shrugged as if to say, 'What on earth is going on here?' My shrug back indicated, 'Your guess is as good as mine, mate!'

Bill fetched us a Coke each from his fridge. 'Here you are, lads, I'll switch the telly on for a while. Just sit back and make yourselves at home. You take the two chairs. I'll sit over here on the bed.' There was a quiz programme being broadcast. Bill said to switch channels if we wanted. I got up from my chair and suddenly realised that I didn't feel right. I managed to change channels on the box but needed to get back to the chair as I felt quite weak in my legs. I slumped back into the chair.

'You look a bit drowsy, lads. It's OK though. I'll turn the gas fire down – it tends to have that effect on my guests.' He got up and fiddled with the fire. 'There, that should do it!'

I watched Dave in the other chair. He wasn't

asleep but he was looking at me with a surprised look. 'I feel drunk, mate. Why should I feel drunk?' Then he giggled.

Bill came over first to Dave and them to me and dropped some magazines in both our laps. Have a look through these, boys. They'll liven you up a bit.' His voice had changed. It sounded coarser, harsher. The magazines were pornographic. I knew now that Dave and myself had been tricked into coming here and we were in danger. I tried to think. That's it! That Coke! We were all right till we drank that. It must have been doped! This bloke had spiked our Cokes!

Bill turned the main light off and lit a small lamp. 'Look mate,' (Dave was trying to sound his usual brave self), 'We're leaving here right now.' He managed to get up from his chair and slowly walk to the door. The door was locked. 'Paul, this nutter has locked us in, do you know that? And he's drugged us or something, I'm sure of it.' Dave was near to tears and obviously realised now we were in danger.

'Look, young David! Sit back in your chair. I'm not about to hurt you. Not, that is, if you just do me a few favours. Reg has helped me a lot and I always pay him. You can see he's not come to any harm can't you? Now, sit down.' Something in this man's voice told me we were in very real danger. 'Dave, do as he says, mate. It'll be all right; just do as he says, then we'll go home.' I turned to this man now. 'Err, Bill, what is the time anyway, my Mum and Dad will have the police out looking for me if it gets too late, you know? And that lad Reg might tell 'em we're here anyway.'

'No, he won't do that, son. He was paid to bring

you here. Look – just take your clothes off for me, then you can go. No harm done, eh?'

'No harm done, you pervert! If my Dad gets hold of you, you're dead. What did you put in our drink, anyway? I might be a kid but you had to drug me, didn't you 'cause you're a coward and we'd be more than a match for you.' Then poor Dave started crying. He cried louder and louder. Now the man was getting concerned about the noise. He went over to Dave and hissed in his ear, 'Shut up, or you'll never go home. Just shut up!' Dave was immediately silent. Then the man pulled Dave to his feet and led him to one of the beds. 'Just lay there and be quiet, understand? You can go home shortly. Now Paul, you get on the other bed.' I went to the other bed. My legs felt like jelly. If I'd wanted to run I would not have got very far. Not only did I feel paralysed with fear, but I also felt partially paralysed from whatever we'd been drugged with.

'Oh, my God! I thought, we are really and truly trapped in here. This bloke is going to kill us. Surely, this was kidnapping. Already he had nothing to lose. Survive, Paul, do what they do in the films. Stall for time. Do anything he asks, but stay alive.' How could I tell Dave this? I'd explained the sex thing before. It was pretty awful from what I recalled. It might be worse this time, but as long as I didn't die, I thought, I just don't want to die.

In the next couple of hours David and I were subjected to the most horrific sexual abuse. At some point, I begged the man to let me use the toilet, figuring that if I could get out on that landing, I'd make a run for it, clothes or no clothes. Bill came out with me. I attempted to struggle past him as we left the toilet. He caught me by the hair and dragged me back into the room. I was shouting and screaming for help. Suddenly he was standing over me. I was back on the bed. Looking up at him, I saw his right arm raised above his head. In his hand was a large brass ornament. It was a Dutch clog. 'Shut up!' he hissed between clenched teeth 'or I'll kill you right now.' He meant it.

'Go on then, do it. I couldn't care less. Kill me, you filthy pig, kill me!' Brave words, but I was terrified.

Suddenly the door crashed in, completely off its hinges. The room was suddenly full of men in uniform and plain clothes as well. The police! No, I wasn't going to die that night after all! Dave and I were taken from the flat and underwent a medical examination by a police surgeon and forensic scientist. It was all dream-like. Surely I was going to wake up and find it was a dream. I told the police surgeon about being doped. I was still feeling the effects of whatever we'd been poisoned with. Next a social worker was called in. It was decided that I would immediately be placed back in care. As far as I recall, Dave was allowed to go home. My father had been informed about what had happened but he never showed his face. This wasn't because he didn't care. It was probably shame, or – didn't he care after all, even after this?

There was a court case some time after the attack. Dave and I were too young in those days to give evidence. But at a preliminary hearing, we had to identify our assailant in Court. No more than that. Many years later, I discovered from one of the officers present at the arrest that Bill had been detained indefinitely at a top security prison hospital. Reg had been using an alias. Apparently Bill had also molested Reg on several occasions and had paid him to lure younger boys to his flat. By some trick of fate, we met Reg, shared a stolen meal with him, and were nearly killed while this pervert satisfied his sexual desires on us.

'That's enough, Dr Miller. You've heard it now as it really happened. Maybe what your report says doesn't exactly match up. But you've heard the truth. If I've never been honest about anything else in my life, these things really happened. I'll say this one last thing, doctor. Every children's home that I went into, I became the object of at least one person's perverted desires. Some of these so-called responsible, caring individuals were aware of my past, the trauma that I'd already suffered, yet they made me a target. In the end, I actually believed that there must be something wrong with me. Was I unconsciously giving off some sign to these people? You see, although there must be thousands like me who went through similar ordeals, it's a very personal experience and you feel that at some time you're the only person on earth that it's happened to. You reach a condition somewhere deep down inside which tells you sooner or later it's bound to happen again. You never expect anything else in the end. You expect to be hurt.'

The doctor stood up and spoke.

'Paul, I'm going to say something to you. In my twenty-odd years in prison work, you're the first prisoner that I've listened to whose experiences have brought me close to tears. In this job, one cannot, for obvious reasons, become emotionally involved with inmates. But the least I can do is recommend a speedy allocation out of Scrubs.

163

You've no doubt heard of a place called Feltham. It's going to be my strong recommendation that, as soon as possible, on the next available draft if I have my way, you are transferred to that establishment.'

On that note, he summoned an officer to come and escort me back to my cell. While we waited, the escorts arrived and the doctor shook my hand. He slipped his other hand into my jacket pocket. On the walk back to the cell, I discovered a twenty packet of fags.

Chapter 17

Time at Feltham

It was Feltham that I was eventually allocated to. Although a closed establishment it was considered relatively easy going and, personally, I found this to be true. On my arrival with about twenty other inmates, the first thing I noticed was that officers didn't wear uniform. The reception routine was far more relaxed. Perhaps, I thought, this wouldn't be so bad after all. Maybe the doctor had done me a favour in pushing my allocation to this place. Only time would tell.

We were gathered in a canteen area, all twenty new arrivals. We'd been fed, and the food was an improvement. Both Ashford and Scrubs had served swill compared to that first evening meal at Feltham.

'Halpin, Potter and Doran. If you would pick up your kits and follow me, please. I'll take you over to induction. The rest of you, don't panic. You'll be collected in twos and threes shortly. We're short-staffed this evening so just hang on and we'll get you settled for the night.' The officer sounded genuinely concerned for the remaining inmates.

We were taken through the prison (it was still prison, as far as I could see, Borstal was just another label given to it) to what was known as the induction wing. It was a smaller version of the wing at The Scrubs. But no one was locked up. Inmates stood around alone or in groups. Some sat watching a TV at one end of the wing. Others stood around a snooker table watching a game that was in progress. The general feeling I was picking up seemed to be, 'so what, another bunch of prisoners had arrived.' We passed a group playing cards at one table, at another, dominoes. It was very noisy in that wing and overcrowded from what I could see.

I was allocated a cell on the second landing. It was just another cell, though painted a little brighter, and the floor was tiled, no floor boards or concrete. An improvement, I thought.

When the officer had shown me to my cell and gone off in pursuit of new arrivals, there was something bothering me, niggling me. Something felt strange. The cell was a little brighter and although barred, the window in the cell was wider and would probably let a lot more natural light in during the day. Then all of a sudden I twigged what was bothering me. The officer hadn't banged the door shut: in fact, it stood wide open. The noise from the ground floor, the raised voices seemingly in competition with the TV which must be up full volume, filtered into the cell through the open door.

I made my bed up ready for the night ahead. I was really tired and was tempted to shut the cell door myself and sleep my first night here away. The din coming from below irritated me. I didn't relish the idea that I would possibly have to associate with that rabble and noise, but I was one of them, after all. Maybe it was just first night nerves. I'd get used to it. I was learning fast that you had to adapt, you had no choice really.

I wandered onto the landing taking with me water jugs and a bowl in search of the recess. Filling my jugs with both hot and cold water and rinsing my washing bowl clean I went back to my cell. Sitting on my bed I waited, what for I don't know. I needed somebody to tell me what to do next. An officer came along then.

'Hello, Halpin. I'm your induction officer. You're no doubt feeling a little lost just now, but that is normal for a new inmate. Most of the officers at Feltham are medical officers, we like to try and treat you as patients rather than prisoners. We do the best we can in a prison environment. It's not easy for us or you, but working together we do as much as possible to treat you as human beings. I can assure you as borstals go, you're in one of the most easy-going establishments. That is, err, where staff are concerned, the relationship between inmates, err, that is, with each other, is a different ball game. My advice to all new inmates is pick your mates carefully.

'You can be here for the full two years or you can toe the line and be out much sooner, in some cases that has been six months. Those inmates who make it in six moths are very few, a rarity. But it can be done. By the way, my name's Mr Andrews. I've been assigned your induction officer. You will be on this wing for a month and then allocated you training house. We call them houses, they're not of course. It sounds better I suppose calling them houses. You're in cell nine, and your prison number is 74922. You're responsible for keeping this cell spotless at all times. I've worked at Scrubs, so I am familiar with that set up. We work differently here.

'We do have a cell inspection every morning, but provided your bed is made up properly every morning at unlocking, we don't have beds turned against the walls. There are penalties for keeping an untidy cell, such as loss of pay or cancelled association. Association is that racket that's going on down there. The biggest penalty is loss of remission. You have no set remission time as a Borstal boy, but myself and other staff assess your progress, and everything from cleanliness to manners is taken into account and will ultimately determine your length of stay. Many rebel against the system and lose out. They remain with us for two years. It's your choice.' At last, he'd finished, well not quite. 'Any questions, lad? Anything you want to ask me?'

'Well sir, I...' He stopped me finishing my question. He said, not unkindly, 'Look, Halpin, I've not been knighted, nor ever will be; cut the "sir" bit out. "Mr Andrews" will do nicely. Now what were you about to ask?' I tried again. 'Well, Mr Andrews, that racket you referred to down there – association you called it – is it for everybody? I mean, do we have to join in, that is, every night?'

'Well, tonight no, but usually I'm afraid so. We have to keep inmates together you see, son. But remember, this is just for a month. Things are different as you move on. Now I've got to move on – other inmates to see. I can pull your door to if you like. They don't bang up here until 8.45. It's just 7.20 now.'

'No, leave it open, Mr Andrews. May as well get used to it, eh?' I said.

'You may as well, son! See you then.' Then he was gone.

It puzzled me how I'd suddenly felt like being my own gaoler. Just a few days ago I'd have done almost anything to keep that door open, and just put up with the noise, or anything else, come to think of it.

I walked out onto the landing, looked down on the inmates below. It was a funny situation not being able to recognise the familiar screws' uniform. They were around, however, perhaps not quite so obviously, but could be picked out in their civilian clothing. One sat near the group of inmates watching TV, another chatting to a gathering of inmates. One had even joined in the card game that was in progress.

'Blow it, I'll have a wander down there,' I muttered to myself. 'Why should I be nervous or afraid of this lot!' because I realised that yes, I was afraid. Nobody else could see that, I hoped, but Paul was scared. I made my way down to the ground floor. Nobody gave me a second glance. Nothing to it, I thought. It's just crossing those barriers of fear. That way I'm going to survive, just as somehow I've always survived no matter what life has thrown at me.

Deciding to join the TV watchers, I found an empty chair and sat down. They were watching Coronation Street and as I glanced around at the audience, it was obvious that each individual was following every piece of the action. There was a commercial break and the audience broke into what sounded like a gaggle of geese communicating with one another. The guy next to me asked if I had a light for his smoke. I had a box of matches in my pocket and gave him a light.

'Would tha like twos op ont ciggy, lad?' he asked me in a northern accent I could understand this bloke's interest in Coronation Street. In real English, what he was asking was if I'd like two's up ('twos up' in prison slang was half of something) on his ciggy. 'Yeah, thanks mate, if you can spare it.' He smoked half of the roll up, then passed it to me. 'Ere ar, lad. Oh, ay up – Street's back ont tellah.' Once again he and the rest of the audience were glued to the set.

What a bunch of morons, I thought. I'm getting up right now. Just look at them, like rabbits caught suddenly in the headlights of an approaching car, unable to move. But I didn't move. I sat through the rest of the programme, with all the other morons! It was light relief. It was uncomplicated entertainment. They weren't the morons I'd first perceived them to be. They were prisoners who sought, like me, freedom of mind – and you used any means to achieve that, including soaps like Coronation Street. I'd learnt another lesson about prison.

At eight o'clock, a trolley was pushed onto the wing. You could help yourself to the cocoa and rolls that were on it. The cocoa was thick and surprisingly sweet. Each person was allowed a pint of cocoa and one roll, though the cocoa could be sold for two ciggies. I watched as several people did this. Cigarettes in an establishment like Feltham could buy you most things. In those days it was prison currency.

The next hour was spent trying to make small talk with the other prisoners. Inevitably, the conversation got around to crime. This subject and the opposite sex were favoured by most inmates. No-one wanted to talk about much else.

It was with relief that the evening's association came to an end and we were called back to our cells.

In the cell now, I listened to my transistor. It was company enough that first evening. People were a pain anyway, I thought, as I lay on my bed. Yet, at the same time, it was only natural that I would need some kind of human contact while I was here. I would just be careful who I made friends with, if there was such a person one could call a friend in these circumstances, that is! Yes, I'd take that officer's advice – I'd pick my mates carefully.

I switched my light out and sought the solace that sleep would bring. It didn't come immediately. I tossed about in the bed for several hours. At one stage, the Judas hole went across. A voice on the other side of the door said 'Goodnight'. I replied the same. Was it an effort for a screw to wish a prisoner 'goodnight', or was it said out of routine? Who knows. It really is a different world in here. Thinking back to my sharing those awful experiences with Dr Miller, it concerned me that these people now knew (the staff, that is) that there would have been a report made. My case notes would be lying in some official's office. How many people would have access to that file?

'Stop fretting, Paul' I told myself out loud. What was done was done. All I needed to do now was work my ticket out of here. Where **was** out for me?

I had no idea. All I knew was I wanted out, the sooner the better. 'God help me' was all I could say. 'If you love me, help me.'

Chapter 18

My Name's Paul and
I'm an Alcoholic

The first two weeks in the Induction Unit of Feltham went by without incident. I was aware that my behaviour was being monitored carefully. Although the staff never actually pushed themselves on me, you were always aware of their presence. This gave me an almost paranoid enthusiasm to get things right, to please them in some way. There were several personal interviews with various staff members, and also group meetings which were made up mostly from the inmates I'd arrived with. Mr Andrews had spent quite a while with me one day, as my induction officer. It seemed he would play an important role as to where I moved on to within the system. He wanted to know more about my drinking and drug taking than anything else. He also hinted that he was aware that I had been a victim of sexual assault, but he very diplomatically spared me the grief of having to go over it all again.

Mr Andrews and I were sitting together in my cell one morning. He asked me outright, 'Do you believe, Paul...' He used my Christian name. This surprised me; after all you didn't get personal with screws, did you? He went on, 'Do you believe, or rather, can you admit, that you are an alcoholic?'

'Well, Mr Andrews, I don't really want to believe that I am. But yes, I'll say that it certainly is a big problem in my life – the biggest problem now being I can't get my hands on the stuff!' This was an attempt at humour. It didn't go down as funny with the screw, however.

'That stuff, as you put it lad, may well be your undoing again and again. You'll need to do something about it while you're in here. You'll need to show a desire to the discharge board that you have tried to help yourself. Your efforts to change, particularly your drinking habits, could influence the discharge board when it comes to a release date. Do you get my drift, lad?'

'Yes, Mr Andrews, I think I do. I'm sorry if it sounded like I was not taking this drink thing seriously. It made me quite ill for a while just before my arrest. I just couldn't cope without it. For some reason, it became more important to me than anything else. Don't ask me why I'm like that. I guess, yes, I'm an alcoholic.'

'Well, if that's the truth, and only **you** can really make that decision for yourself, you need quite seriously to seek help.' He stalled a while. I didn't know how I should reply. Saying the wrong thing might jeopardise my being released sooner rather than later. Finally, I found the words that maybe he wanted to hear.

'Mr Andrews, I'll accept any help I can while I'm here. I do want to change, really I do. To be truthful, to discover you're an alcoholic so young – well, you picture alcoholics as old men in rainmacs and long dirty beards – it's hard to take on board, if you get my meaning.'

'Yes, I can understand what you've just said. Bearing in mind I'm not an alcoholic, let's put it this way. If someone has cancer, the medical profession can offer treatment – you know, drugs and such – but at the end of the day, who really understands cancer? What it feels like, how it not only affects a person physically, but the effect on that person's mind knowing that they might die well before their time would naturally be up. What do you think?'

'Well, er, um, I suppose another sufferer would really understand best.' I didn't want to sound smug, but I needed to get this man and any other staff I could on my side. This was the obvious answer to give.

'Good, that sounds very near the right answer.' He didn't say anything for a while. I was quite sure he was waiting for me to make the next move, so I did.

'Where will I find help here then, Mr Andrews? I'm willing to go into therapy or whatever they call it. I'll try anything.' Whether I really meant these words didn't matter. It was my freedom that was at stake here, not the screws'.

'Have you heard of an organisation called AA, Alcoholics Anonymous?' the prison officer asked me.

'Can't say I have, Mr Andrews' was my reply.

'Well, there is a meeting here on Fridays, in the evening at seven o'clock. We allow a couple of members of that group to hold a meeting here, for prisoners with drink and drug problems. Would you like to give them a try? You've nothing to lose by going.' He paused, then added, 'Take my advice – give it a go.'

I said I would go.

That following Friday I attended my first meeting of AA. The meeting was opened by one of three civilians in a classroom situated in the education department of Feltham. Although an officer escorted us, there were three of us from induction. No screws were actually present in the classroom; just a handful of prisoners and the three civilians, two male and one female.

One of the male civilians, Joe, opened the meeting. 'My name is Joe and I am an alcoholic.' He then went on to share his experience as a practising alcoholic and his life today as a recovering one.

I was amazed as this man shared his life with us inmates and even more amazed at how I was able to identify so much with his drinking habits, even though he was twice my age. He spoke a lot about God. He didn't say anything about Jesus, but he believed that God and only God could have restored him to sanity and that if any of us really sought God for ourselves, and with the help of other sufferers of addiction, we could recover from this illness. It was an illness, a three-fold illness, physical, mental and spiritual. How can you be spiritually sick? I wondered.

I continued listening to Joe. Here was another human who really understood where I was at. He had been there. Maybe there was hope. After all, there were people like me out there somewhere. I wasn't alone.

The meeting finished with a prayer, which we could read from a poster they had brought with them. It was called 'The Serenity Prayer':

'God grant me the serenity
To accept the things I cannot change,
The courage to change the things I can
And the wisdom to know the difference.'

After the meeting, tea and coffee were provided. I went up to the man, Joe. 'My name's Paul and I'm an alcoholic. I'm glad I came tonight, Joe. One thing bothers me, though. How does this spiritual sickness bit fit in, and who says it's an illness at all?' Suddenly I was quite bold in addressing another person. It occurred to me that I'd also admitted (from my heart) to another human being that I was an alcoholic.

Joe's answer was direct and made a lot of sense. 'The medical profession for a long time now, Paul, have recognised alcoholism as being a disease, a killer disease. It was slowly killing me and thousands of others like me and has already killed many others, both old and young and from every race and class. It's my belief that we are not just physical beings, but we also have a spirit. Look, perhaps it would be better at this stage not to complicate things with the spiritual side of it. Keep it simple – seek God in prayer daily asking him to reveal his Spirit in you. If you have a Bible, read it. I'm not a Christian myself, but I believe in a power which I call God. I'm still searching for a deeper meaning to that: meanwhile, I keep an open mind.'

In my cell that night, I contemplated the events of the meeting. The thing that really bothered me was that it seemed at sixteen years of age I was an alcoholic! Why couldn't I just be normal like other teenagers? Then again, what was normal anyway? Normal people seemed quite boring. Normal people didn't end up in prisons either, I told myself. Maybe boring wasn't so bad after all!

Somehow, at this stage I couldn't or wouldn't give in to the idea that I was an alcoholic. After all, by the time this place is through with me, I thought, I'll have been alcohol-free for quite a while. This was my way of getting around admitting defeat, but I knew that the staff here had to think I'd cracked it, that I'd accepted it, accepted that I was, and am, an alcoholic. I'd fool them, go along with this AA stuff. Maybe when I'm older, I'll really need to go there. I mean, sixteen really was too young to be labelled a hopeless drunk. Yes, I'd gone over the top for a while, drink had got me into this mess, but when I was released, it would be different. I, Paul Halpin, would be the exception to the rule. A few drinks now and again, maybe a joint or two as well. But no more crime; this was it. I'd cruise through this sentence, 'Yes, Sir', 'No, Sir', keep my nose clean, then freedom and a completely new start.

I felt quite cheerful right then. There was hope. I was going to be all right!

I wrote two letters that night, one to my dad and the other to my mum, telling them that it really wasn't that bad in these places, that the staff were good people who were going to help me sort my life out, and the food was very good as well (I knew the mail was censored so a bit of flattery wouldn't go amiss).

As I wrote, it suddenly dawned on me that we (my parents and I) didn't really know each other. It was like writing to a couple of strangers. I went from feeling optimistic about my plight to feeling quite empty and sad. I was tempted to tear the letters up – after all, what did they care anyway. I resisted the impulse, the letters would be sent. Finishing the letters, I signed off with the words 'Your son, Paul.' It seemed a lie to write this. I was an imposter. Still the letters had killed a bit of time, if nothing else. Then I went to bed. Another day done, I thought. How many more to go? It didn't bear thinking about. I willed myself to sleep. Sleep brought temporary release. One day I'd really be free.

The next day was Saturday. At 11 am, a film was shown in the gymnasium. Almost the whole Borstal population came together for this 'privilege'. It was also an occasion that for me would bring trouble.

The film was a comedy, one of those 'Carry On' films. It was amusing and a welcome distraction from everyday Borstal routine. About half-way through the first half of the film, something or rather someone, flicked my ear. It stung and caused me to turn quickly behind me. I looked at the two most likely offenders who sat directly behind me. They both met my gaze with looks of apparent complete innocence. One of them spoke.

'Got a problem, mate?'

Then the other, 'Lost something, or what, pal?'

Facing the screen again I decided not to react. I didn't need, nor did I want, any trouble.

It happened again a few moments later, this time both ears receiving a stinging flick.

Turning slowly this time, I confronted the same pair.

'Pack it in,' I said.

The looked at each other, then back at me.

Again, they both spoke.

'Pack what in, mate?' one said.

179

'Yeah, pack what in?' said the other.

'You know what' I replied. Then, 'Just leave it out!'

I faced the screen again. I'd lost interest in the film. It happened again, flick, flick, in succession. My fists clenched in anger. Flick, flick again. I spun around in my chair, almost knocking the guy next to me off his chair, aiming my right fist first at the face of one, then the other. Both punches connected. The lad to my right fell to the floor, clutching his nose. The other, although stunned, lunged towards me. The gymnasium suddenly lit up. The film went off. My antagonizer and I rolled around together on the floor. Someone was bleeding. I wasn't sure if it was my blood or his on the floor. It was on my hands as well. I was aware of shouting and cheering, cheering; for me or the other inmate I didn't know. Probably just the sight of blood and a brawl – that would be enough, I supposed.

Suddenly hands grabbed me and hauled me to my feet. My right arm went up my back. In this position I was marched out of the gym – not back to my cell, but to the Chokey. On the way I protested my innocence and screamed at the officer that he was breaking my arm and that if he would let go I could explain. He wasn't taking any notice. Arriving at the Chokey, the punishment cells that is, I was shoved into one of its special lock-ups and the door slammed shut behind me.

On Monday morning, the Governor of Feltham came to my cell in the punishment block. I explained to her what had happened and why I had struck out the way I had. She had to believe me, as I knew such behaviour could result in my being in this place longer than need be. Mrs Ellis, the governor, listened to my explanation. When I'd finished, she said her piece.

'You struck two inmates. I accept you were provoked by these two lads, but we cannot condone violence of any nature at this establishment. Harris and Grimes have both admitted that they wound you up. Your version of the incident seems to be the truth. I'm going to give you a caution this time. However, you will remain here in the punishment cells for another twenty-four hours. So will the other two. Give you time to cool off. Any more of this violent behaviour, Halpin, and you will pay dearly, understand?' She looked sternly at me as she said this.

'Yes, Ma'am – I'm sorry – it won't happen again' was my reply.

Chapter 19

A Call To Surrender

Back at the Induction Wing, I really began to throw myself into working myself out of this place. OK, I'd had a minor hiccup but I would make up for it. Somehow, the incident at the gymnasium had to be played down.

My allocation day was here. The Board and its members were in agreement that North House was best suited to me. It contained mostly inmates with drink or drug addictions. The assault in the gymnasium was briefly mentioned but on account of my good behaviour otherwise, it would not affect my progress towards my eventual release into society. What a relief I felt when hearing the Governor say those words!

So I was transferred to North House. The first surprise on arriving there was that I was given a choice of sleeping quarters: a cell or a shared dormitory. I chose a cell. If I had to live with others, that was fine – I'd put up with that and they could put up with me – but I wasn't sleeping with them as well. It turned out to be a wise choice as from now on I would only have to sleep in my cell at night as inmates here were all allocated work during the day.

My work was to be in the gardens of the Institution. It suited me down to the ground! My boss was a friendly individual with the very fitting name for his chosen career as a gardener. It was Mr Tree. He took me under his wing and taught me so much about plants and vegetables that I could have used this experience later on in life, I'm quite sure.

Life in the Wing was also quite bearable. The two inmates I'd scrapped with were in the same Wing. I never had another set-to with them. There was, it seemed, a kind of respect towards me. The fact that I'd proved myself someone not to be messed with had paid off. Being in the gardens most days kept me away from the crowd. I was discovering that really I was quite a solitary person. There was a great comfort in physical work. It was a new thing for me. I worked hard, always in the back of my mind wanting to gain my freedom.

I still attended AA meetings, not so much for its philosophy but in search of God. Yes, I realised that there was a need in me, quite a hungry one, to really find God. Also I attended church services on Sundays, even went to Communion. To a certain degree I knew it was 'front': it was what the system needed to see, but there was also a determination, a searching going on within, a desire to change, to make something of myself.

My Mum and Dad were writing and occasionally sending money. It was a start. It must have been a sacrifice. My Mum couldn't possibly have very much and Dad would drink most of what he had usually, so perhaps we did have something between

183

us after all. In one of my Mum's letters she even offered to put me up for a while when I was eventually released. This thrilled me, as it was impossible to be freed without having secure accommodation to go to. Yes, I thought, things were beginning to look up. There really was light at the end of the tunnel.

North House, being what it was (a Wing for addicts) was not completely drug-free. Prisoners would always, no matter how secure the regime, find ways to smuggle drugs onto the Wing. Half an ounce of tobacco would purchase enough cannabis or a couple of amphetamines with which one could get high. Like most of the other inmates, I eventually gave in to temptation. At the end of the day, although I never got caught, there was an awareness every time I took a drug, of being a failure. I hadn't beaten my addictive personality. It was easier to push that part of my nature deeper into obscurity. Deep down I was still in denial of the fact that I was an addict.

At one particular AA meeting, one of the visitors was sharing that as long as we were in any degree of denial towards our addiction, we wouldn't beat it. It would master us. She also said that unless we completely gave our will and lives over into the care of God, our spiritual lives as well as the practical, wouldn't get right. We all needed God but he never forces his love on anyone. God gave everyone free will, to choose his way or our own. Before we went back to the Wing that night I cornered the female visitor. Her name was Barbara.

'Who is your God, Barbara?' I asked her.

'Well, I'm a Christian. But I come to AA because it's with other alcoholics and drug addicts that I'm understood. And it's through this fellowship that I found Jesus. Another alchy shared with me her conversion to Christ and, not immediately but after a lot of searching and doubting I might add, I surrendered and let Jesus have his way in my life. I've not taken a drink or a drug since. AA is not my God, but for me has been used as an instrument of God. Does that answer your question? Paul you said your name was. Is that right?' she asked.

'Yeah, Barbara, that's right. That more or less answers my question' was my reply. As I stood next to this woman, something stirred within me. There was a presence about her which made me feel uncomfortable. I felt guilty, convicted. The fact that I'd smoked a joint that very morning in one of the greenhouses at work came to mind. Making my excuses, I made to leave. She stopped me before I could escape. She asked me if I had a Bible of my own and if I would allow her to send one in to me if I didn't. My answer was that there were Bibles around – but no, I didn't have my own. She took my name and number and said she would post me one.

That night, I prayed to God to give me what that woman had. She seemed so content, so at peace. But there was more than that, she made me feel, or rather, she had an aura – a presence – about her that seemed to touch the hidden truth that I hadn't stopped taking things to get a buzz. That night my whole miserable life seemed to flash through my mind, even the fags I smoked seemed somehow a horrible thing. I began to toy with the idea that this woman was indeed touched by something that was good and clean and everything that I wasn't. I said the Serenity Prayer out loud several times.

When I eventually slept, I dreamed again of my past. A strange man kept coming into the dream. He never said anything – just seemed to be there with that same presence about him which the woman at the meeting had. At one moment he just looked at me and smiled ... the dream finished. Waking the next day, looking around me, I somehow expected someone to be there in the cell with me, someone smiling.

True to her word, a couple of days later the promised Bible arrived. Inside the front cover was inscribed these words:

> 'To Paul. There is only one way to God and that is through Jesus. I'm praying that one day you'll find this truth for yourself. Keep on searching and God who sees your heart will honour your searching. Jesus wants to free the innermost depths of your soul. You cannot hide from God. He knows everything about you.
> Love in Jesus' Name,
> Babs, AA'

I read the Bible every day. I'd read a chapter or two before going to sleep. Most of it was beyond me, especially the Old Testament. I continued with AA as well. Barbara came several times to the meetings. At one meeting she shared with me about being born again. Just like Nicodemus in John's gospel, I just couldn't understand how I could be 'born again'.

'It hasn't got anything to do with a physical birth, Paul. It's being born with God. In a sense you have to die a spiritual death and then you receive God's Spirit – then you'll understand. Don't struggle with it. If you're open to God, in **his** timing he'll lead you to that point. Keep it simple. God loves you, Paul. He doesn't love your sin, but he really does love you. Just remember that. He loves you as you are, but too much to let you stay that way.'

That night in my cell I struggled with my feelings like never before. Why did I always have to ask questions about God? Why couldn't God just change me there and then? Why all the searching? Why, why, why? Couldn't I just become calm and peaceful like that woman?

The answer was there. I knew it. In my heart, getting high was still something I wanted. I was still smoking joints, feeling quite smug about not getting caught. Really, I liked the risk of getting caught, although I liked to think they would never catch me. Anyway, booze was my problem, not dope. Always compromising to make it acceptable – that's me! I'd never change.

As I read my Bible that night, every verse seemed to be about how useless life without God was, how the things that gave our flesh pleasure were in fact a barrier that came between us and God – including dope and booze, I supposed.

Trying the age-old argument with myself that God himself – well, Jesus anyway, the Son of God – turned water into wine. Then, the realisation that the Bible didn't say anything about God turning people into drunks either. 'OK, OK, God, You win,' I said out loud. 'I cannot blame you for my addiction. But I'm finding this really difficult.'

The word 'surrender' flashed through my mind. The key for me to unlock the real prison I was in was that word, 'surrender'. To put my hands up and surrender ... to whom? Not to the prison system. Not to AA. Who to, then? God? Surely, I'd done that. I'm reading the Bible. I'm praying. I'm smoking dope. Bang! It struck somewhere deep inside. Exactly – you're smoking dope! No complete surrender, Paul. Compromise always, just like before. God, on your terms, just like everything else. If I'm smoking dope in here, what chance will I stand where the booze is concerned, where it's available on every street corner? If I defend the dope smoking, in reality it was just a replacement for now, until I could get my hands on a bottle. Jesus, I just can't let go.

'No, Paul' a voice in my head spoke, 'Not can't. Won't!'

The word 'won't' reverberated around my head. The voice belonged with a face, a person. It was a person who smiled at me in dreams, and really knew me with that smile. My reluctance to respond to the person who smiled was baffling, I thought.

Then the voice again, 'No, Paul, not baffling. Surrender, remember, surrender, no compromise. All or nothing.'

Going to sleep that night, it now occurred to me that becoming a Christian for me wasn't easy. I was complacent in my ways. It wouldn't be much trouble to just throw the whole idea out completely. A cop-out attitude, just like I'd copped out of everything else in my life. If it required effort on my part, I could and would look for an easier way.

I'd always considered, deep down that is, that religion, particularly Christianity and Jesus was for wimps. I was beginning to feel like the wimp in all this. How weak I was and, yes, how full of pride I was. Maybe I'll do something about it tomorrow. Meanwhile, I'd sleep on it. My final waking thought that night was that God was on my case. I wasn't sure if I liked that!

Chapter 20

A False Sense of Freedom

Six months went past, and every month my case was reviewed. The first five months without my being present. On this, my sixth month into the sentence, I was requested to attend. The other inmates were winding me up, telling me things like 'we've seen the results,' and that 'your name has been recommended for release.' It wasn't so. When I entered the room where the discharge board sat, it was like being in court again. My work reports were excellent. The fight I'd had was not mentioned. Mr Tree, my works instructor in the gardens, had given me a glowing report and, yes, he had actually recommended an early discharge. However, the wing report had really let me down. The wing officers all seemed to agree that I was secretive, to the point of being anti-social. They were under the impression I may have been taking drugs. They all recommended further training was required. One officer even requested I be moved from single cell accommodation to the dormitory.

The governor always had the final say. 'On this occasion, Halpin, you will not receive a date of discharge. Anything you'd like to say to us, the board?' She awaited my answer.

'Well, yes, Ma'am. I'm not quite sure where the officers get the impression from that I'm using drugs. That seems unfair: surely there has to be proof to back up a statement like that.' I regretted opening my mouth. I realised it sounded like a challenge. Too late, I thought. It was out.

'Halpin, my officers all have a medical training which includes a study of the effects of certain illegal substances when taken by an individual. I trust their judgment 100%. I'll say no more than that.' Then she dismissed me from the room.

The following day I was moved to a dormitory. What had happened? Someone must have it in for me, informed on me for smoking dope – the lads who I had whacked that time? Surely not. I was getting on with them more than anyone else. Maybe this was God's doing – that was it! – my punishment for smoking dope. All right, have it your way, God. No more dope. You win. Just get me out of here! As for being anti-social, who was I supposed to socialise with? The only things that inmates talked about were sex and drugs and rock and roll – oh, not forgetting crime. What a joke! Surely my going to AA should have gone in my favour and my mother had written just recently repeating her offer to come and stay with her. I was a loser, even in here, a loser.

That night, my first night in the dorm, my bed was sandwiched between a snorer and a non-stop wind-breaker. I'd tried to read my Bible before lights out, but gave up after persistent interruptions from the snorer and wind-breaker. The one who became known as the snorer had been given his discharge date. He was being released in two weeks and wanted me to know about all the wonderful things he planned to do on his first day. That bloke never knew how close he came to ending his life that very night. I had to restrain myself from throttling him!

It became a relief to get off the wing every morning and into the gardens and greenhouses. I'd thanked Mr Tree for the discharge recommendation. He wasn't really a screw. He was a civilian instructor and I supposed he saw things differently. He said that he couldn't see how I was anti-social. Besides, he said, anti-social types don't have green fingers like I had. It was a pleasant consolation to hear these words. I'd not give in: somehow I would just keep going.

On the last day of September, 1980, just a week after my seventeenth birthday, the discharge board gave me a release date for 17th October. I'd have served about ten months of a possible two years. At last, the end was in sight! All I needed to do was keep my nose clean for a few more weeks.

On the morning of my discharge, I was taken early to reception. I was given a jacket and trousers, shirt and tie to put on. My original clothing had been destroyed. While dressing in a special discharge room, the reception officer gave me the items of property taken from me when I'd first arrived. Among the items was the expensive watch I'd bought with my ill-gotten gains. He also gave me a pair of new shoes and a small blue holdall. It contained toiletries and underwear, he said. Finally, a brown envelope was handed to me. In it was my train ticket to Watford, £17 discharge grant and some official documents stating my release conditions, etc.

Then I was walked to the gate by an officer. Signing my name in a book was the last thing I needed to do before the gate was swung open and I walked free. The officer pointed to the margin in the book where I was to sign. This done, the officer motioned me through the gate. As the gate shut behind me, instant relief flooded through me as I looked around the street I stood in, thinking 'What shall I do next?' 'Anything you like,' I thought, anything you like!'

Heading towards the local British Rail station my head reeled – and something else, I felt out of place. I was sure that everyone that passed me was looking knowingly. They could smell the Institution on me. It showed in the way I walked, even the way I looked. Scared is how I felt, really scared. The moment I'd dreamt about for so long, and it was frightening! This wasn't how it should be. In the movies the ex-con. is met at the gates of the gaol by his sweetheart. They run towards each other. The movie goes into slow motion as they come together. Their faces tell it all. The moment they've been waiting for has arrived...

It was all a bit of a let-down, I thought, as the train station came into sight. Not even a relative to meet me, let alone a sweetheart. I boarded the train going to main line London, having to change trains at one stop for Euston which was the station required to get me across to Watford.

The fear had now subsided – still a little uneasy, but it was to be expected, I supposed.

Arriving at Euston with 45 minutes to kill before the Watford train came in I went for a coffee.

Surrounded by commuters mostly, I sipped my drink. What would it be like staying with my mum – after all, we were strangers in many ways. It was going to take some adjusting, and she'd got this bloke with her. Still, without the offer she'd made, I'd have been 'no fixed abode' and then the system would have put me in some hostel of their choice. No way! – this was best for now. I'd take a stroll around the station. This lot I'm surrounded by look like robots, I thought.

Passing the station bar, I stopped to have a look in, just a look mind. After all, I didn't drink any more, did I? Not like before, anyway. That was just too much, before. Must never let it get the better of me again. Anyway, couldn't I just walk away from this bar now? No real need even to go in. I've got 20 minutes left before my train goes. Quick half, as they say. Well, I'm hardly going to get drunk in 20 minutes, am I? It'll settle my nerves. 'One quick drink' I told myself as I walked through the door and up to the bar.

'A pint, please.' I laid my hand on the beer tap of my choice. The barman nodded and poured the pint. I paid him and took the beer to a table nearer the door, wanting to watch the world go by. Several drinks later, still watching the world go by, I realised my train had gone. Well, so what? Plenty of trains after that one. Another beer won't hurt anyway. No whisky though; definitely no whisky! Strictly a beer person now – that was me. Wasn't I a reformed character? Just a few more beers, then I'd definitely board the next train, no bother.

Arriving at my mother's house much the worse for drink at six that evening, I was given a cool reception.

'Had a drink to celebrate then, have we?' she asked as she stood back from the front door to let me in.

'Yeah, just a few Mum. Felt a bit nervous, like. Not used to it all just yet. But I won't make a habit of it, promise you that. No, I've learnt my lesson now. Gonna get a proper job first thing tomorrow, pay my way like normal folk.' Not really sure that I meant these words.

'Well, you can start paying your way now. Give me a fiver towards your keep. There's a meal in the oven if you want it.' Giving her the fiver from what was left of my money, I headed for the kitchen, heated the meal up, sat at the table and ate it.

My mother watched me from where she sat in one of the worn armchairs. Looking around the room we were in, it was obvious that my mother was really quite poor. My mother was no better off than me. I'd try to help her if nothing else. I would just take it easy with the booze. Besides, the probation officer who had been assigned to oversee my progress back in civvy street wanted to see me the next day. (I'd been released on licence for the remainder of my sentence.) I'd have to keep him happy, otherwise he could have me sent back to finish the whole two years. My mother, I'm sure, had only offered the place as a home so I could get out sooner than later. She'd even lied about where I would sleep, saying that I'd have my own room. I wouldn't over-stay my welcome. She obviously had enough on her plate without me being around.

My mother told me that if I went out that night to be in by 11.30. After that, the door would be locked. Then she told me, with some effort, how she wished it could be better for me, but it was all she could offer. She added that the sofa was to be my bed.

Needless to say, I got drunk that night. If I'd learned anything from my time away, it didn't seem like much. I'd put on a bit of weight; that's about all. Borstal had been a waste of time. I was back to square one.

Making it back to my Mum's just before 11.30, she heard me come in.

'Is that you, Paul?' she called down the stairs.

'Yeah, it's me, Mum. Shall I bolt the door?' I called back up.

'Yes, and switch the lights off,' she answered.

I locked the back door I'd come in through and lay down on the settee fully clothed. A blanket had been left to cover myself with. Tomorrow I'd leave. This wasn't my home. It never had been. My family were complete strangers. I'd see the probation officer tomorrow. Maybe he could find somewhere else. The drink I'd taken did its job that night. It rendered me unconscious. When I awoke, it was still dark. Switching on the light, I looked at my watch – 5.30 am. I felt quite hung-over. Gathering up my bag which contained my few possessions, I left the house. 'No' I said out loud. 'That wasn't my home. It was nobody's fault, but it just wasn't where I should be. Neither did I belong there.'

Back in the street, I wandered for an hour or two. The thought crossed my mind that maybe I'd have been better off back in the nick. At least I had a reason to get up in the morning. Passing a corner shop which I knew sold booze, I went in and bought a bottle of plonk. Nothing had changed. My old friend (or enemy, whichever way I wanted to look at it) was always ready to come to the rescue. Need to be careful, though – my date with the probation officer was at two o'clock. I didn't want to turn up drunk.

In the town centre now, I went into the public loos, locked myself in a cubicle and drank from the bottle.

Well, I thought, so much for freedom. Here I am sitting on a toilet seat, drinking wine at six o'clock in the morning. My money was running out as well. I'd need to do something about that.

Another walk around the streets killed another few hours. It wasn't good enough. I didn't even have a friend. I walked to the graveyard, found one of the old school there and shared my wine with him. He was company at least.

I arrived at the probation office on time. I'd purchased some strong mints to camouflage the smell of drink, though I'm sure he still detected it. I told him (Mr Butcher) that being at my Mum's was probably a big mistake, that maybe Watford was not the place for me.

'Look, Paul, I'm a fair man. There will be no pressure put on you. It's difficult for you just now. If, however, you don't stay at your mother's, please let me know of your whereabouts and try to leave the bottle alone. Call in to see me once a week to start with. Just come in. If I'm not around, the receptionist will let you know when to call back. Now, is there anything you need right now?' He finished.

'I've given most of my money to my Mum, Mr Butcher, so until I've arranged some help from the DHSS, I'm broke. Is there any chance of a loan?' I seized the opportunity while it was going.

'Yes, just this once, maybe we can. I'll speak to

my supervisor, see what we have in petty cash.' He got up and left the room we were seated in. He was back shortly asking me to sign for £20.

'It's not a loan as such, more of a subsistence for a recently released person. You won't have to pay it back this time. Now what I suggest you do while there's still time is to pop around to the Social Security, if you have your discharge papers with you. Do you have them?'

I nodded 'yes.'

'Good, they should be able to help you as well – financially, that is, until you get a job. You will be looking for work, I take it?' he asked.

'Oh, yes. Soon as I'm settled, I'll be out there looking. I'll get around to the DHSS then, and, err, thanks for the help. See you next week.'

He showed me out of the office and I headed for the DHSS.

The DHSS gave me another £25, but I wouldn't receive any more for a fortnight. I never told them about the money from Mr Butcher. Already I was breaking the law. It was all too easy to forget about what was right or what was wrong. For now I wouldn't give myself a hard time about anything. If God wanted to do so, that I couldn't stop. But for now I'd take my chances with or without God.

Chapter 21

Just a Couple of Drinks to Celebrate

There was only one way my life could go as long as I continued to kid myself about the alcohol, and that was down. Over the next six months, I continued to drink. Petty crime on a daily basis became the norm. Mr Butcher, my PO, had already given me a warning about my lifestyle – that if things didn't change soon he would have to revoke my licence and take me back to court for breach of conditions.

For a while, I turned back to God, not that I'd ever truly found him, but rebellion would surface and I just wouldn't surrender to him. Still, it had to be on my terms. AA wasn't working, even though many recovered drinkers offered the hand of friendship and support. Always, my selfish pride told me that Paul knew best and I'd do it my way.

I'd persuaded my mother to lie to the probation after-care service and tell them I still lived there. In fact, I would crash out at different squats around the town, occasionally spending one night at mum's

199

to make it seem half true, for her peace of mind rather than mine.

Now I was using speed (amphetamines) on a regular basis on top of the booze. I kept telling myself if I could just get through the after-care bit, I'd feel free to really get my life sorted out. It was as though I'd never left gaol at all. One day at a meeting with Mr Butcher, I shared that with him. He told me that it was within his power to cancel the licence at any time, which would let me off the hook, but I had to show that I'd made some kind of way forward. He was willing to make a deal with me. If I went into voluntary treatment for my addiction for three months, he would arrange for the licence period to finish early. Reluctantly, I agreed. A place was found for me at a local clinic. For three months I miraculously stuck it out. People including doctors and shrinks were convinced that Paul was a changed man. They helped me find a flat to live in, offered me on-going counselling. They couldn't do enough for me.

My way of repaying them, now that as agreed I was freed from my obligation of Borstal after-care, was to turn the beautiful home (probably the first place I'd ever known as home) into a den of vice. You could come to Paul's flat as long as you had something to offer – sex, drugs, booze. There were parties every night which went on right into the following day, sometimes even longer. The police were regular visitors because of the racket and violence which would break out when people were stoned out of their minds. Personally, I was arrested several times during this period, but unlike in the past, I no longer admitted anything and so kept out of prison for a while at least. But my luck would eventually run out. Really, I was desperately unhappy and very sick from drink, and now drugs as well.

By the year 1974, although still hanging on to the flat, I went crawling back to AA. I was about twenty years old now and had almost fatally over-dosed on drugs and booze several times. Going to meetings almost every night kept me sober physic-ally but there was a condition around AA known as being a dry drunk. Yes, I stayed sober but did nothing else. After six months of this, I'd saved up quite a bit of money. One evening I decided that I'd have a nice Indian curry and a bottle of sparkling wine. After all, this was the proper way to drink, wasn't it? Who was I kidding?! Within days, I was drinking around the clock again.

People had told me time and time again, 'to let go and let God,' 'that alcoholism was an illness, a progressive illness.' I couldn't take it on board, why on earth not? Anyone who put himself and others through hell and torment had to be sick, a complete nut case. I began hearing voices and was convinced that people were coming to kill me. One of the voices would tell me, quite audibly, that I didn't need a God or Jesus, that in fact I was God. Yes, I was insane when I look back now. Paul Halpin was over the top.

People were avoiding me (I wonder why?) as now I was preaching that if people would only listen to me, I'd show them the real meaning of life. This was always done bottle of wine in hand of course, unless my funds went to stronger stuff. Even the local park bench drinkers, who I'd got on well with in the past, avoided me if possible. I began to carry a knife to protect myself, from no-one in particular, but definitely someone was out there waiting to kill me – but I would get them first.

The police picked me up one night, or rather the early hours of a Sunday morning, and conveyed me to the local mental unit. They said I was a danger to myself, rather than others. Apparently, a concerned member of the public had rung them when I'd rung his doorbell (a complete stranger) and said that I was an SAS officer and that the IRA were staked out in his back garden, and that I had come to flush them out. This incident led me to being sectioned under the Mental Health Act. While in hospital on this occasion, I met another patient, an Indian lady. Somehow, she would always try to sit next to me around the ward. At first, I thought she also was planning to kill me, like everyone else. But no – this woman spoke to me one day. As she spoke, a memory flickered through my confused mind. The woman had the same presence about her that Barbara had (the woman alcoholic from AA). She asked me my name. I told her. At first I thought that she might be just an hallucination. But as she spoke about Jesus – she was a born again Christian – a peace, a clarity seemed to form in my mind. For a moment, I wanted to get away from her. There was something in me that didn't want to hear what she was saying; then she made a statement that seemed to penetrate my whole being: 'God has a plan for your life. You may or may not be able to physically or mentally comprehend that now. But he loves you, Paul. You have never known love from humans, but you will one day look back on all the horrors of life and know that everything you've been through, everything you will go through in future, God has been there. He has already revealed himself to you in ways that only you can recall.'

As she spoke, I saw myself crying and asking Jesus to heal my tooth – I was back in the Convent. She went on . . . 'Give in to God, Paul. Surrender to Jesus.' She was quiet for a while. Her lips moved but she was quiet. 'I'll pray for you.' Then she left me.

She never approached me again whilst I was a patient at that hospital. But from then on I got well. My medication was reduced and finally stopped completely. Jesus? God? Who knows? One of the consultants at the hospital called me into his office one day.

'You seem to have responded to medication, young man. Remarkable really. Thought you might be with us for much longer. People suffering alcoholic psychosis sometimes never recover. You're very fortunate. What's the secret then, eh?'

I didn't answer. All I did know was that it was something to do with that strange woman. No, not just her – Barbara as well – and the healing of my tooth as a child, not forgetting the preachers who had visited the prison. Something was growing: a seed had been planted many years ago in that Convent. I couldn't see it just now, but one day it would make some sort of sense. A week later the Section was lifted.

The flat had gone; been repossessed and all my belongings taken for the rent I owed.

Making a big mistake, I went to my dad's house. I started to go to the pub with him, only drinking Coke. Everything in me said 'keep away from pubs,' but still I went. It was the company I went for, not the booze, I lied to myself.

One night I met Eileen. She would eventually become my wife. She was attractive and, more important, showed me affection, something that was missing from my life. Although she drank alcohol, I still only drank Coke. We decided to get married, just like that! We wrongly believed we were in love, the truth being that we were both lonely and vulnerable people who were in love with the idea of being in love. In November 1975 we were married. We had no money, no real home of our own, just ourselves. We moved into a bedsit in the town centre. I shared with her the problem I had with drink and why I only drank Coke. She said she understood, but couldn't I have a drink now and again?

'Maybe in a while' (the lie again – I was back on dangerous ground) was my reply.

Eileen was Irish. She wanted to enjoy life. We went to a party together one night. Some time that evening, I drank a beer, then another, then a glass of wine. A couple of joints were passed around, I took a few drags. That night I went home smashed – we both did.

Next day, although desperate for a drink, I resisted. I went back to AA. It helped for a few weeks. Then I got a job in an engineering factory. My wife also found work in another factory close by. It felt good to wake up sober and go off to do something useful. We had money to pay our bills and to spare. My wife had made some friends at work. She would go out with them a couple of nights a week while I stopped in or went to AA. Alone in the bedsit, I would get bored. At these times, I often thought about God and Jesus, even praying that I could be a social drinker. Surely, I was a man, now twenty-one. All the bad things were behind me. I needed a reward for all my hard work at the factory. Just one night out a week for a pint or two wouldn't hurt, would it?!

The next pay day, I announced to my wife my plans to have a night out with her friends.

'But you make sure that I only have a few beers, OK?' I said. She agreed to keep her eye on me.

Of course, it never worked. We both rolled home plastered. Going to work the following morning, hung over, I really craved the hair of the dog that bit me. There was a shop near the factory that served early morning drinkers. Purchasing two cans of strong lager, I took them into work with me. I went into the men's loo and drank them. Now I could get on with the day. At lunch time, instead of having lunch with the lads at work, I headed for a nearby pub and got drunk. Needless to say, there was no more work that day, or the next. Paul was back on the spiral, downhill all the way. The booze once more took a firm grip. Eileen, my wife, started to show concern. She would now learn the hard truth about alcoholism and living with an alcoholic.

'Why can't you just have a few drinks like me. You've no willpower, that's your problem,' she would say. Or, 'You've started drinking spirits again. They don't agree with you. Just stick to beer, then you'll be fine.' She didn't have a clue.

I never returned to that job but managed somehow to get other jobs; always the same thing would happen – I'd go on a bender.

Days were now being spent with the down-and-outs again. My wife complained that I was beginning to smell and wouldn't let me into her bed. I slept on the sofa. She, my own wife, could no longer leave her purse lying around as I stole money from her for drink. Instead of going home now, I began to sleep out with the wino's. Some of them were not sure about me as I'd been crazy in the past. They kept away from me, but other crazies understood me. We sought out each other's company. For a while, Eileen would come out looking for me and drag me home and try to clean me up. Within days, after making all sorts of promises to Eileen and God and Jesus, I'd drink again. In desperation one morning, I drank my aftershave lotion, then my wife's perfume. In desperation herself now, my wife took me to a doctor. He examined me, then gave me pills to combat the DTs. Also he said, 'If you don't stop drinking you'll be dead in three months. Your liver is already damaged. It's your life. There's nothing any doctor can do. You've already had one Section Order. That may happen again. Perhaps you won't come out of it this time.'

Tough words, but the truth. But **still** I drank. Again, I began stealing, not caring whether I would get caught. More important was the booze.

One night I broke into some offices and got caught. Bail was refused. Three weeks later I was brought before the magistrates and sent to prison for a year. My wife waited for me while I served eight months of that sentence. Again, I made all the usual promises to stop drinking.

The day of my release my wife met me at the gates of the prison. While I'd been away, we had been allocated a council house on one of the estates. We both believed this would be the turning point in our lives. For a while, I didn't drink. Again returning to AA, I got a job with a local builder as a labourer, but I drank again, lost the job, went back to crime and was soon caught again. The judge gave me two years. I'm convinced today that those times in prison actually saved my life. Locked away, there was no alcohol. I've even considered that it was God's mercy that I was there. While in prison this time, my wife and I decided it was pointless going on together. We were divorced. Eileen returned to Ireland. We never saw each other again.

Chapter 22

The Prison of Addiction

For me, there were two prisons: being released from one, which was the prison of locked doors and barred windows, I would enter the prison of addiction, the latter being the harder to free myself from.

When I was released from the latest gaol term, nothing had really changed. In many ways, I wanted to turn around and go straight back to the solitude of my lonely little cell. So I just drank and took drugs. No home to go to, I became a drifter, a tramp. I went back to London and drifted through the parks and other meeting places for down-and-outs, spending most nights along the embankment or under the arches at Charing Cross. Time was immaterial. I never knew the time, or even the day, when blacked out on drink and drugs. I spent countless nights in the drunk cells. Occasionally, the Salvation Army would take me in to one of their hostels and dry me out. Some of them would, like others in the past, tell me how much Jesus still loved me, despite the condition my life was in.

There was a man around in these days who slept

under the arches at Charing Cross, a Christian who had chosen to live among the tramps and runaways. He really seemed to have a genuine acceptance of the men and women around him and they, likewise, accepted him. He would talk about Jesus, only if you wanted, but unlike many of the Christians who would come to such places, he also wanted to know you as a person and not walk away as soon as you showed a lack of interest in the faith he had. Basically, he was a good listener, not just a preacher. He took a space next to me one night under the arches. He offered me a drink of coffee from a flask he carried with him. Declining the offer, I suggested he have some of my wine instead. 'No thank you,' he said, 'not a drinker myself.'

'Not a drinker? Then why are you down here then, with us?' I was curious – and suspicious as I asked him this.

'Well, put it this way – by the way, my name's John – Bible John – that's my nickname. What's yours?' He offered his hand in a greeting. 'As I was saying ... A long time ago, I asked myself a question. "If Jesus were alive in the flesh today, and someone came and asked me his whereabouts and could I help them in finding him, where would I start looking?" Oh, I am sorry, friend, didn't get your name' he interrupted himself.

'Paul's my name. You sure you won't have a drink?' It would have made me feel a little more at ease if he was drinking, like everyone else. And yet this character did seem to somehow blend in with the flotsam and jetsam he was surrounded by.

'Now, where was I? Ah, yes!' he went on. 'Well, it occurred to me that I might send that someone to the local churches or the Bishop's house, somewhere like that. But guess what? The most likely place for him to be found would have been down here, with you lot, or in another place like it. He loved people like this.' He indicated with a wave of his hand the scrap heap of humanity around him. 'So, Paul, that's why I'm down here with you' he finished.

'Hang on a second, John, no, just hang on a tick while I have another swig of my wine. Then I'll be with you.' Having had my swig, I asked him this: 'John are you trying to tell me that you're Jesus, or what? If you are, then you must be on something. You sure that coffee's not laced with brandy or whisky? I tell you what – if it is, I'll have some, then you can be anyone you like!' I laughed at my own joke. John laughed with me. He wasn't offended. I really liked this man.

'No, Paul,' he continued, 'Jesus is unique. God made him that way. The reason I'm down here is that I just want to be like him as much as I can. I'm not perfect, Paul; far from it. Only Jesus had a right to that claim. Another thing, I'd never be able to live down here in my own strength. Jesus is with me; he strengthens me to come here. Are you in any way a believer, Paul?' he asked.

'Oh, I don't know, John. Sometimes things have happened in the past that make me want to believe. I'm not really sure at the moment.' I took another drink. Then another and another. Then I must have crashed out, waking at about 4 am. 'Bible John' had gone. Before he'd gone, he had given me a pocket size New Testament. I left it on the ground where I'd slept and went in search of more drink.

By now I was having fits. One moment I was conscious; next I would wake up in hospital or just wherever I'd fallen. It occurred to me that this happened more when there was a lack of alcohol in my system. They were identical to the symptoms of epilepsy. One of the hospitals I'd been a patient in gave me a calling card for a day centre in the West End of London where treatment was available from a special clinic for homeless addicts. Also, a meal was available and showers.

I began to use this place on a daily basis. The medical team there were very caring. The doctor who first saw me told me all the usual things: one, that my liver was enlarged; two, that no-one could help me until I wanted to help myself; and three, that if the drinking didn't stop, I would possibly live for a year if I was lucky, or I might just end up with a wet brain and spend the rest of my life a cabbage. Medication was supplied for withdrawals and for the convulsions I was having. The doctor explained that I would probably have them from time to time, especially when (through circumstances not of my making!) no alcohol was available. The pills should help.

The doctor had also made available, if I wanted, access to an alcohol unit. For now, I declined.

I was a regular visitor to Pentonville Prison hospital wing. Magistrates would send me there on a regular basis for drink-related offences – begging, criminal damage, shop-lifting, etc. It was on one of these visits to Pentonville that I learned about 'Jack drinking'. 'Jack' was the common name for meths and surgical spirit. These alcohol-based chemicals were very cheap. For a pound one could stay drunk for a couple of days. I soon became a member of that exclusive club of drinkers.

I was dying – of that there was no doubt! One day

I was found by a couple of lads in a derelict house in East London. They phoned for an ambulance. I was unconscious: they thought I might be dead. At Barts Hospital in London, I went through the most horrendous withdrawals despite the huge doses of medication. I went into convulsions which nearly killed me. Through the pain and delirium, once again a voice, not my own, was echoing in my alcohol-soaked brain, 'Surrender, Paul' and then a vision – the smiling compassionate man, nothing more, just the smiling compassionate man.

I agreed to go into long-term treatment and was transferred to St Bernards' Hospital in Southall. I remained there for just eight weeks. In that time, I built myself up physically. Long-term treatment would normally have been six months to a year. Again, Paul knew best. Now I was cured, I believed. I'd experienced near-death and was quite sure this was enough to stop me drinking. It wasn't.

Soon I was back on the street, heading for a certain early grave. I'd even begun to desire death – just to die – to close my eyes and die. I was a no-hoper. No-one, not even the smiling compassionate man in my vision, could help me. Death was the only way out.

Chapter 23

'Dead On Arrival'

I didn't want to live, neither did I want to die really, so I remained in the hell of addiction. My only reprieve was the local prison which had become like home to me. Also I was now convinced that these forced periods of sobriety kept me alive. During one of these reprieves I began praying again, only this time there was a desperation. The discovery that no human power could help this individual was now very apparent. I drifted back into Watford for a while having just served another six months in gaol. I looked almost human; when I arrived at my Mum's she put me up for a while but again it just didn't work out. I didn't fit in with the other members of the family that stayed there. I really wanted to, but always felt rejected no matter how hard I tried. If ever there was a black sheep I must be blackest of all.

Drifting back to the street I drank again. Mostly I drank alone having imaginary conversations with any character I wished. And I prayed, or rather just talked to God about this and that. I was a lonely, destitute figure. I begged for money in the street to subsidise my DSS money. I still stole from shops, usually from supermarkets which stocked drink. Eventually every large supermarket in Watford, rather than prosecute me when they caught me, just barred me from the shop. I was known to every store detective in Watford.

I didn't know it then, but God was about to enter into my life for real. It seemed that wherever I went, God would place someone in my path. Christians would approach me on park benches and tell me about Christ and how he was wanting so much for me to totally give myself to him. They all mentioned that the key to entering into that very special relationship with God was to surrender my life, warts and all, over to Jesus. I would then receive forgiveness and, more importantly, salvation. I would be saved!

Whenever I passed a church with a service in progress, drunk or sober, an irresistible urge to go in would come over me. I would steal into a seat close to an exit as I would sometimes be filled with a overwhelming sense of conviction and have to run out of the church. But still, drink mastered me and I couldn't put the bottle down.

One day I decided that life was no longer worth living. I would die an alcoholic, maybe God would let that happen anyway and put me out of my misery. In the summer of 1979, having just been released from another gaol sentence, I decided to kill myself. This overwhelming feeling of wanting out of it all tormented me day and night. One day while drinking surgical spirit, a voice in my head told me quite clearly the time had come to finish it. I broke the now empty bottle of surgical spirit on the ground in front of me. Picking up a piece of broken glass with my right hand I slashed at my left arm. This took place in a local park. A couple rushed over to me when they saw what I was doing. Another member of public phoned for an ambulance. I spent two days in hospital and was then discharged with my arm stitched and bandaged. This method of suicide was far too messy, I thought. Besides, the hospital hadn't taken it as a serious attempt, they thought I was just a drunk crying out for help. They told me that what I really needed to do was to stop drinking.

I registered with a doctor and managed to con him into giving me a large quantity of a drug called hemeneverin. It was to help me come off alcohol. The doctor warned me that to drink on top of the drug could be fatal.

I was living in a derelict house close to the town centre. The next day I collected my DSS money and went to an off-licence and stocked up with several bottles of whisky. I had two bottles of the drugs with me. This time I would do the job properly. On returning to the derelict house it was my intention to drink my last drink on this earth. Sitting on the mattress which was my bed, I proceeded to drink the whisky. Then I just took a few of the pills. I drank some more whisky. My whole miserable existence flashed before my eyes. It was hopeless. I couldn't salvage one period of my whole life that I thought worth going on for.

Some time later, one bottle of whisky finished and one bottle of pills down my throat, it occurred to me that if I wanted to stop this I would have to act quickly. The last thing I recall was trying to get up from the mattress. My legs wouldn't support me. I was really going to die before anybody found me!

I felt myself drifting. Another effort to get up failed. I took what I believed was going to be my last drink, shut my eyes and waited for death. I felt myself disappear into a black tunnel.

'Mr Halpin. Paul. Mr Halpin, are you there? Are you with us?' Someone calling me. But I'm dead, I thought. Then a face, my eyes were open. There was a face. Oriental, Chinese. The devil, maybe. If I was dead, I wouldn't be in heaven. Too wicked by far. Definitely a Chinese face looking at me. 'Mr Halpin, do you know where you are?'

The face talking to me. Wearing glasses? The devil wearing glasses? A Chinese devil? Not quite the expected demon with horns.

'You're in hospital, Paul. I'm a doctor.'

So, I wasn't dead after all! I remembered I was supposed to be though. How did I get here? Closed my eyes, slipped back, back to wherever I'd just come from. Unconsciousness again. Oblivion.

Forty-eight hours later I regained full consciousness, feeling like death warmed up, but there was no doubt I was alive. Moving about to feel if all my limbs were intact, I found tubes inserted in almost every orifice of my body: arms, legs and one or two in more painful places. One of the tubes went from my arms to a saline drip hanging from a stand at the side of the hospital bed.

'Hello, Paul,' the face now with a body attached addressed me. He was Chinese, definitely not the devil but a doctor it seemed. 'Do you remember anything about all this? You were in a bad way when you came in. Do you recall anything at all? Just nod if you can hear clearly and see properly.' I tried to speak but he stopped me, so I just nodded as he'd said.

'Now, don't try to speak, Mr Halpin. Just listen. You, young man, are very, very fortunate to still be here in the land of the living. The amount of alcohol alone could have proven fatal to most men, and with the hemeneverin tablets as well, it's a morgue you should be in, very much dead.'

He paused to shine a light in my eyes, and place a stethoscope on my chest. He went on.

'Do you believe in God in any way, young man? Well, whether you do or don't, perhaps you'd better start, because someone up there' (he looked heavenwards) 'must like you a lot! I'll leave you to mull that one over. By the way,' he lifted up my arm as he spoke, 'Do you see this?' He moved my arm in front of my eyes so I could see the hospital identity bracelet. On it, I could make out my name, a date and the abbreviation 'DOA'. I nodded that I could indeed see it. He exclaimed, 'DOA normally stands for 'Date of Admittance.' In your case consider 'Dead on Arrival' more appropriate. You'll never get another chance like you've just had, young man. You are in every sense of the word a miracle.' Then he left me with those words hanging in the air.

Me a miracle? I thought. This mess of a human being a miracle? This was a hard one to take on board. Where then do I go from here? I didn't have any friends, no family as such, and yet why was I still alive? So mixed up, I'm so confused. Some miracle!

A nurse was by my bed. 'Do you think you might be able to eat something, Paul?'

'Not right now, but at supper time.'

'I'll have a meal brought up with the other ward meals if you like. It's 2.30 now. Supper's a couple of hours away but I'll need to arrange something now.'

She was young, early twenties, maybe a bit younger. I said I'd like some food.

'Good, I'll arrange that then,' she said cheerfully. Then 'Would you like to sit up – see a bit of what's going on around you?'

'Yes, I'll sit up. Thanks, nurse. By the way, when can I get rid of these?' I indicated the tubes and drip.

As she helped me into a sitting position, she informed me that the drip and other lines would probably remain in for another day or two. 'They'll do a better job than dyno-rod; clean all that muck out of your system. A bit uncomfortable in the process but you had an enormous amount of toxins in your system. The doctor probably told you, you are a very fortunate man to be alive.'

She gave the pillows one final shake and pummelling. Then she moved on to another patient.

The supper arrived. I made an attempt at eating it. What went down very quickly wanted to come back up just as fast. I willed myself to keep what I'd eaten down and pushed the remainder away.

'Not hungry after all then, Paul?' The nurse was back.

'Err, well, err, to be quite honest, I feel a bit queasy. Sorry about that,' I said.

'No problem. I'll take it away.' Then she went off again. My eyes wandered around the ward. Not much to look at really – just a lot of sick people. Still, I thought, I'm warm and, yes, alive. Why I don't know, and don't understand, but alive.

My eyes were drawn to the bedside locker. Amid the water jug and other hospital utensils was an envelope. Picking it up I saw my name was printed on the front.

'A get well card?' I chuckled at the most unlikely chance! In fact it was a Bible tract, one of those that people from churches shoved in your hand when around the town. It read:

> *'For God loved* Paul *so much* (the word 'world' had been crossed out and my name put in its place) *that He gave His only Son that if* Paul *believes in Him, he may not die but have eternal life.'*
> (John 3:16)

There was a Gideon's New Testament on the locker as well. I looked up the scripture I'd just read. Then looked around the ward, curious as to who had left the card. None of the patients looked capable of much movement at all. It had to be a nurse or doctor then. Nice thought, especially personalising it like that. Nurses were sometimes called angels. Maybe a real one existed on the ward!

The night staff had replaced the previous working shift. Different nurses were now settling patients down for the night. A nurse gave me some medication. The strange thing was I didn't feel the need for any. Apart from feeling slightly sick and a little shaky I felt quite well. This puzzled me, but I took the medicine anyway. Doctor's orders and all that, I thought.

I slept that night like I'd never slept before, a deep peaceful sleep. Yes, I was glad to be alive. Maybe a miracle had taken place. At least I was off the streets. I wasn't in prison and I wasn't drinking or taking drugs. It was 1979. I was twenty-four years of age and despite my previous lifestyle, God might actually love me. There was hope after all.

Chapter 24

An Angel On the Ward

The tubes came out and the drip came down a couple of days later. This brought on a panic attack. Did this mean I would be getting the boot? I was afraid as never before about facing life in the world. 'It is safe in here' I thought, 'safe from drink, safe from people.' The nurse saw the look of concern on my face.

'What's wrong, Paul? This is what you wanted, surely?' she said. 'I'll put them back in if you like.'

'Oh, no, it's not that. Glad to get rid of that lot.' Looking at her face I decided she might be understanding. So I went on, 'I've got nowhere to go, if they discharge me, you see nurse – that's the real problem.'

'Well, you let God sort that out. And I can assure you you're not ready to go yet anyway. However, if you want to get out of bed now, you can. Take it very easy, though. You'll feel very weak for a while. Your body's taken a real hammering.' She looked at me. 'By the way, you looked at the envelope – the Bible scripture – I'm glad.' She smiled.

'That was you, was it? Yes, it helped. Not sure how, but thanks, it helped. What's your name?' I asked.

'My name's Rachel. I'm a Christian. I'd like to spend more time with you talking about that but nurses are not allowed to spend too much time with one patient. I'll tell you this, though, I'm praying for you. So are a lot of others. If you don't mind, I'd like to speak to the pastor of my church about you. Can I do that?'

'If you think it'll help me, yes of course tell him what you like.'

'Good. One more thing: if you can, pray for yourself. Do that as well. God has got plans for you, Paul. We are going to see you saved through all this. God told me so. Must go now. See you soon.' She went off to see to her other patients.

Proper little Florence Nightingale, that one, I thought. Yet she was extremely confident about God and being saved. At least I now knew where the envelope had come from.

And now I could relax again. She had said they wouldn't discharge me yet. My mind was clearing now. I'd have to start working out a plan of some sort. Meanwhile I'd take Nurse Rachel's advice and let God sort things out.

Rachel came back. 'I'm just about to finish my shift, Paul. If you want, and you've plenty of time, have a look in the New Testament. Matthew chapter 6. Read from verse 26. See you!' She went away again.

I'll get up and walk about a bit, I thought. It wasn't easy. My legs were like jelly, but I managed a trip to the loo and back. I'd been passing water through a tube into a bag before. It was a pleasure to just go to the toilet normally again.

I was beginning to feel giddy, so I got back into the bed again. I picked up the New Testament. Matthew chapter 6, she had said – let's take a look. I began reading from verse 26. It was all about not worrying, about God knowing just what we need. The final verse is what I hung onto. Verse 34 said:

> *'Do not worry about tomorrow; it will have enough worries of its own. There is no need to add to the troubles each day brings.'*

It reminded me of one of AA's slogans about just staying sober one day at a time. I felt comforted. Maybe the Bible made sense of my situation after all. Maybe I'd give Jesus a shot. After all, Jesus may well have saved me from killing myself. It seemed that way right now. What other explanation was there?

The Chinese doctor came to see me a couple of hours later. He explained that I'd be in for a while longer yet. He knew about my homelessness. 'Not to worry' he said. 'We'll get Social Services onto it. We won't discharge you with nowhere to go, although if we eventually need the bed things might be different. Meanwhile, just rest and take the medication being given.'

One thing puzzled me. I seized this chance to clear my mind. 'Doctor, can you fill me in about something that's been on my mind?' He was listening, so I went on. 'Who was actually responsible for my being found and went for help? I'm quite sure I was on my own in that derelict house. None of the other down-and-outs slept there. It's been on my mind.'

'Let's have a look at your case notes. There should be some information along the lines of how you came to be admitted.'

He went away and fetched some notes. 'Ah! Here we are. A John Doyle found you. He recognised you as one of the town's drunks, thought you were dead and rang the emergency services. When asked what he was doing in the building, he couldn't really explain. He said he just felt an urge to go in. Mr Doyle refused to accompany the ambulance to hospital. A footnote at the end of the report says "Mr Doyle was himself very drunk." So there you are! One drunk saving another drunk's life. They do say, Paul, that God moves in mysterious ways his wonders to perform. A classic example of that statement in reality! I still reckon on a miracle, and that drunken gentleman was part of it. Someone up there more than likes you. He or she must like you an awful lot! Must go now – finish my round.'

John Doyle – yes, I'd met John on the Green by St Mary's, Watford. Shared a bottle with him several times. Well, I'm blowed. That really is a miracle – it's got to be. Why me, Lord God? Why me? Suddenly, I was filled with the most overwhelming relief. I was so glad to be alive. Despite everything that had happened, it was good to breathe, to think, to be able to see. For the first time in my life, I couldn't quite put my finger on it, there was hope. Life could at last be worth living.

The next day I had an unexpected visitor. I'd fallen asleep after lunch when I awoke. Someone was sitting by my bed – a man.

'Hello, who are you? What do you want?' He was a stranger – at least, his face wasn't familiar.

'My name's Gordon. Gordon Hickson. Captain Gordon Hickson of the Guided Weapons Regiment. I've been sitting here a while praying for you, Paul. The Lord has sent me to make you an offer you can't refuse.' He sounded very posh, and confident.

'Lord **Who** has sent you? What are you talking about? What offer do you mean?'

'I'm one of the people who has been praying for you. There are others as well. God had told us that we are to give you a home. You haven't got anywhere to live, have you?'

I looked at him. Was there a psychiatric unit attached to this hospital somewhere? If so, maybe this guy with the public school accent had gone missing from it.

'I'm not mad, Paul.' He must have realised what I must be thinking judging by the way he looked. 'The Lord I'm referring to is Jesus. Rachel, the nurse that works here, told us about you. We – that is my Church and family – want to offer you our love and friendship, but most of all we believe that you will come to know Jesus as your personal friend and Saviour.'

This young army officer then shared his testimony with me. He had served ten years as officer-in-charge of operations in a part of Northern Ireland known as bandit country. He was about to resign his commission as an army officer in obedience to God. I had actually spent some time in the part of Ireland he spoke of. I was impressed that this man, who surely must have seen quite a bit of the seedy side of life in the army, could talk so unashamedly about his complete trust and faith, that Jesus had spoken to him clearly about his life and that he should leave the army and serve God in a different kind of army – the Christian one.

This man went on to tell me of his experiences in Ulster, but most of all, he wanted to share Jesus with me. There was a difference in the way he spoke about his faith. Never had I heard such a matter-of-fact approach to what God could do to change a person. I found myself actually beginning to believe that what this guy was saying was for real. After all, why me? What was a commissioned army officer doing even spending the time of day with a waster like me? He knew a little about me, but what would happen when he discovered my past? I was a convicted criminal many times over, a drunk. We'd see how much of a Christian he was, and his family was, once they knew the whole story. Who could possibly want to befriend me?

'What about this offer, then – somewhere to live. Why are you going to all this bother? And what's in it for you and this family? I mean, it's a nice thing to offer a tramp, an alcoholic one at that, a home, but believe me, mate, do you really know what you're taking on board?'

My questions didn't seem to bother him. His reply was again full of confidence. 'We might not know fully what we are doing, Paul, but God does, and I don't believe this meeting is coincidental. God has a purpose for it in both our lives. Oh! And about that offer, not just the home we've talked about, but the fact that God is offering you salvation, freedom in a way you've never known before through Jesus. Let me pray for you now, Paul, then

I'll see the doctors and nurses about getting you discharged from here.'

His prayer was quite simple. He prayed that soon, if not now, I would respond to God's calling upon my life; that I would come to know the love of Jesus.

He went away to find a nurse about securing my discharge. A little while later, he was back with a smile on his face. 'I'll pick you up tomorrow, Paul, and take you to your new family. Are you willing to take that first step?'

'All right, then, if you're sure about all this,' I answered. Then he went out of the Ward.

Well, I thought, what did I have to lose. Where else would I go, anyway? I'd give it a try. After all, I could always back out if I wanted. My street nature was telling me to play it cool but something else was happening as well. I wanted to trust this man. This was a new experience. How could I ever trust anybody? But at least there was a small desire to trust. Tomorrow would tell and I would wait and see.

So this would be my last day in the safety of the hospital. This thought frightened me a bit. I was going somewhere to be with people who didn't know me, and I didn't know them. I whispered a prayer to this Jesus who was still not real to me. But I thought it would be nice to have such confidence and faith as Nurse Rachel and that young army officer. Maybe if I stick around people like them, something might rub off. I'd give it a shot – see where it led. What about the booze? Could I really beat it this time? Maybe this was my last chance. If God was really in all this, and it seemed some supernatural force was at work, I couldn't deny the reality that I'd been almost dead. Something had happened, that was for sure, and it certainly wasn't anything I'd done! I'd done nothing to deserve this break in life. It was too good to be true.

'An offer you can't refuse.' I repeated out loud the words that Gordon had spoken. The offer of a home was easy enough to accept. But Jesus? Salvation? In a way I thought I knew Jesus and God. But it seemed there was more to it than that. It seemed a way of life for Gordon. Could it be for me as well? Could it, Jesus? If so, all right, show me what to do next. It's your move!

Chapter 25

Discovering God's Love Through People

Gordon was back as promised the next day. The nurses had got me up that morning and encouraged me to walk about the ward a bit. I helped distribute early morning drinks to the other patients. My hands trembled slightly but apart from that I seemed to have made a complete recovery.

Gordon and I left the hospital together. I was wearing the same clothes I'd been found in. They were rough, to say the least. I felt scruffy sitting in the passenger seat of the car next to the well-dressed, well-spoken army officer.

We arrived at a nice house in Kings Langley, a few miles from Watford. A sign on the house said 'The Elms'. We went to the door at the front of the house and were greeted at the door by a tall man in glasses. He put both his arms around me and said, 'Bless you, Paul, and welcome to our home.' I was lost for words. It was a long time since anybody had hugged me like that. The man with the hug was Alan Vincent, Pastor of what was then Garston

Church. His wife, Eileen, was there also. She gave me a hug as well. I wasn't sure if I was going to cope with all this lovey-dovey stuff: it was all new to me, quite alien to what I'd been used to. I was introduced to David, their youngest son, then Rachel, their daughter and finally the older son, Duncan. Someone handed me a cup of coffee. I was thinking, 'What happens next?' I was completely out of my depth. I took in my surroundings and the people. They were a family. What does one do around a proper family? As for me, I didn't have a clue. At that moment, I wanted to run away. This wasn't for me. I didn't belong here. There was an overpowering presence in that house, in these people, that threatened to suffocate me. After a while, I realised it was a thing called love. It was on their faces, in their smiles. It seemed even to come out of the walls and furniture. It was both human and supernatural but I knew it was love. The thing I'd been denied all my life was now overwhelming me. No-one had to say anything to me – it was just there. To this very day, I'll never forget what happened inside me; something broke, and I suddenly knew without a doubt that there was a God, that he was love. Jesus was in that house, in those people. They radiated the love of Jesus. I wanted to say that there and then, but words wouldn't come. I kept it to myself.

Then they prayed for me. They all gathered around me laying hands on me. I marvelled that I didn't resist, secretly hoping that some powerful presence would enter me and stay with me. Someone was making funny noises – no – they were speaking in a strange accent. Sounded Russian or something like it. Later on, I was to discover that this was called the Gift of Tongues.

It was all very strange. I'd been taken from a life of drunkenness and crime. Suddenly, I was surrounded by people who really did care about me. They gave me clothes and fed me and not once did anyone ask for anything back. Their love was the unconditional love of God. For the first few days, I basked in this new experience. If I'm honest, I was still feeling suspicious about it all and expected it to turn into – I don't know what – the feeling that some demand would be made of me sooner or later. After all, everybody wants something back eventually, that's for sure.

It never came. After a while, I started to offer to take Tuppy, their family dog, for walks in the fields at the back of the house. I would take these opportunities to pray to God and to thank him for what he was doing for me. Still, I was mystified and occasionally became doubtful about these people. But they just kept on loving me.

They took me to their church on Sundays. That was an experience in itself. To be quite honest, my first visit was spent just looking around me at these people. They danced and sang with complete abandonment. They'd never get me at that carry-on, I thought. But another side of me wanted so much to join in. I envied their freedom. This crazy lot had awakened in me a spiritual hunger. I wanted what they had. My secret prayer was that God would show me how to get the freedom these people had. On that first visit, at one point in their worship they all started talking and some even singing in that strange language of spiritual tongues. What on earth is going on in my life?

What was I doing here? However, crazy though they seemed, I felt at home. Each time I went to church I began to feel more and more at home. But still something was missing. There was something everybody else had that was not so obvious in my own life as in the others in the church. This freedom to sing and even dance baffled me, even embarrassed me. In a way, I considered all this singing and dancing a bit silly. What had it all got to do with my life? People would often just come over to me in church and pray for me. Often they would say that God had revealed something specific about me to them, and amazingly enough they were often spot on with what it was.

I'm not sure that I was ready for all this.

Alan Vincent asked me after one Sunday morning meeting what I thought about the church. All I could say was, 'It's certainly different.' This, for whatever reason, caused him to burst into laughter.

A couple of months passed. Life at The Elms was comfortable. Somehow though, I couldn't, or maybe wouldn't, respond wholeheartedly to Alan and his family with the same love they showed me. It was as though I was waiting for the bubble to burst. Eventually, they would reject me. Why should these people be any different? I would search Alan's face for any tell-tale signs that his love towards me was dwindling. In a way I had a perverse desire to actually find something. Needless to say, it was never there. Once, when Alan and I were alone in the lounge, he in his favourite armchair, I sitting opposite on the settee stroking Tuppy, I looked up from my petting the dog and looked across at Alan. His eyes met mine. He was crying.

'What's up, Alan?' I asked.

'There isn't anything up, Paul. I was just sitting here thinking how much Jesus loves you, and how much we love you. You're special to us.' Then he went quiet again.

My reaction to these words was to say that Tuppy needed a walk and I got out of there as quickly as I could. He meant every word. The problem was I just couldn't cope with being loved like that. Would I ever be able to love others like that? More like – did I ever want to?! At times like this, walking in the fields with Tuppy, I would think up ways to get them, that is the Vincents, to stop loving me, to reject me. It would be much easier that way. Rejection and disappointment had been the norm for my whole life. This love thing unsettled me. For the first time since I'd been discharged from the hospital, I wanted to blot everything out.

It was agreed that I would do some chores as a contribution towards my keep. I started to do jobs in the garden of The Elms, also some jobs around the church. It kept me busy, but still I had this growing desire to run away. There was a certain amount of discipline required of me, and Alan and Eileen also in a loving way had brought in a Christian discipline. They disapproved of my smoking so that had to go, though I still had a crafty puff now and again. Although they didn't see it, I'm quite sure they knew. The family atmosphere was still alien to me. Sometimes Alan or Eileen seemed to know that I was struggling. I found it hard to be honest with them about my struggles. There were even times when I thought about booze. This loving family of God just kept on praying for me.

233

One Sunday, we went to church as usual. Normally, I tried to keep to the back of the building. This Sunday found me in one of the front rows. As the church began to fill up, something was different around me or in me; I wasn't sure – both probably.

Someone nudged me. 'Hi, Paul, you remember me?'

A voice spoke, a girl's voice. I looked at the speaker. A familiar face, but I couldn't quite put a name to it.

'Rachel, you know, the nurse with the mysterious envelope. Lovely to see you here!' she said.

'Oh, yes, sorry Rachel. I'm coming along fine, really fine. Didn't recognise you out of uniform.'

We were interrupted with the announcement that praise and worship was about to begin. Away they all went, singing, clapping and one or two even dancing in the aisle. I stood there and half-heartedly clapped, afraid to really let myself go. I remembered the prisoner who had stood up in the prison chapel and cried. It was the same fear I had now. Concerned about what others might think, that kept me from joining in. It's all right for them, I thought. They've all been Christians for ages, some of them all their lives probably. I'm not sure that I'm really one of them anyway.

The Pastor was talking now. The musicians had stopped playing and all eyes and ears listened to the sermon he was preaching. For some reason, I felt uncomfortable. My heart seemed to be beating quite fast. I had a sensation of expectation.

The sermon had finished. Alan took a seat. One of the other leaders of the church was talking into the microphone about unsaved people. My heart beat even faster. He went on about today being the day of salvation, that at least one person in the church today was hearing God's prompting to surrender all, to give in completely. My heart was making my knees knock together. Was he talking to me? That word 'surrender' frightened me. The speaker asked us all to close our eyes. Then he invited any unsaved people to stand before God in repentance and receive the gift of salvation. My eyes were shut tight. I wanted to do this thing. Whatever it was that God had to offer at that moment, I wanted it. I couldn't prise myself from my seat. Then the smiling compassionate face was once again in my mind so clearly that it was as if he was standing there. I got to my feet, unsure what I was really doing. My concentration was on that smiling image. There was nothing to fear, it seemed to say, then it was gone. My mouth opened and the words just came out, 'Lord Jesus, I really don't know what's happening here, but I need your forgiveness. I'd always thought myself a believer of some sort; maybe I've got you all wrong. Lord, I surrender my life to you today. I want you to be my Friend and Saviour.'

Then I opened my eyes to find I was the only person standing. The church suddenly erupted into a chorus of Alleluias. 'Crikey,' I thought, 'What have I done?' Rachel the nurse was crying. She threw her arms around me saying, 'You've done it, Paul. Welcome to the family of God. You're saved. You're a Christian now. You're born again. You're an answer to prayer, you really are.'

Then she went back to praying and singing along with the others. There hadn't been a bolt of lightning or anything like it. All I know is that something important had happened to me that day.

If I had ever thought that being a Christian was an easy life, I was about to discover that I was entering a battlefield, not so much a physical one but a spiritual one. My life as a believer had just begun, but for me it was to be a tough beginning. In many respects, I was entering into the hardest years of my life in that I really had to die now to the old Paul. Jesus couldn't force me to do anything. I had free will just the same. But the first step had been taken. Paul Halpin had surrendered; the first and most important battle had been won.

Before God and man I'd asked forgiveness for my sins and I had really meant what I'd just done. The journey had begun but somehow I knew that the need to cling fast to God and his people was really the key to reaching the final destination.

Chapter 26

Love Is *Very* Patient

Three weeks later, I was baptised at Garston. It was step two for me in my new-found Christian life. At the baptism service, I gave a short testimony before being fully submerged in water. When I came up out of the baptism pool, I prayed out loud in tongues for the first time. I'd received my first spiritual gift from God. What I'd believed would never happen had become a reality for me as well. Now I also began to sing, dance and clap in services. What I'd discovered was the freedom to worship God openly. No longer did I worry about other people, or what they might think. God loved me; it was him I was dancing and singing to, not man.

God began to do a work in me that was at times very painful. My first year was one of learning. Most of all I found it hard to accept discipline and this got me into many scrapes around the Vincent household. Sadly, I drank again but God was always there to pull me back when I cried out to him.

Again and again I rejected the love of Alan and Eileen Vincent but they never rejected me. They had the most amazing patience and love for me. Being a Christian meant hard work. At times I felt everything should be done for me. Really I was being shown by God how to grow up.

One day I took myself back to the streets with a preconceived idea that I could save all the other drunks and drug addicts. I ended up drinking and taking drugs with them. God picked me up, dusted me down and forgave me. It was forgiving myself that I found really hard.

Again and again I rebelled against what God was now quite firmly doing in my life. I couldn't get away.

There was one occasion when I gave in completely. I stopped praying and made excuses to miss church. Alan and Eileen were also now becoming quite firm. They still loved me. They warned me after one drinking bout that if I thought that I could have one foot in the world and the other in the church I was heading for trouble, and that I needed to be in one camp or the other, not both. I chose the world. I make no excuses when I look back. I thought I could muck God's people about. By doing that it was God I was hurting. Alan went off to India and left me in the care of Alan and Val Stevens. I took advantage of his absence by going off on a drinking spree which led me back into crime. I broke into The Elms – the very place which God had given me refuge in – my first real home. Surely they would reject me now! The police eventually arrested me in Alan Vincent's car which another man was driving. We had taken the car from Alan's garage, put Tuppy in the back seat and went for a drunken drive.

When I came to in the police cells, hungover and full of guilt, I was convinced that God would never take me back and certainly Alan and the family would wipe their hands of me.

'Mr Halpin,' the gaoler had come into the cell, 'Who owns the dog that was with you? He needs to be collected.'

Explaining that Alan and Eileen were in India, I suggested they contact Gordon Hickson; he would know what to do. Gordon came to the police station and tried to secure my bail. Even now they were willing to give me another chance and forgive me.

Alas, I went back to prison. Alan and Eileen never stopped loving me. They came to visit me in prison. On my release, they were there to receive me yet again. Only this time, they made it quite clear that I had to get right with God. My problem was I wanted to be a Christian but I didn't want to be a responsible one. I've learnt the hard way that this doesn't work.

I had another drinking bout while staying with Alan and Val Stevens. Alan Vincent was called to the house. What happened next was to be the turning point and probably the making of me as a Christian – not that I saw it like that at the time! They packed my bags and had some prayer with me, then Alan Vincent walked me to the front door, and in a voice full of emotion, this is what he told me:

'Paul, we love you, but it's because we love you that you need to be put out of this house. You've rebelled again and again.'

239

He paused to look at me. There were tears in his eyes. He went on:

'Do you remember the story of the prodigal son?'

I said I did.

'Right then, at the moment, your heart is in the world. That prodigal son of the Bible ended up living among pigs and eating pig swill.

Go back into the world. When you've eaten enough pig swill, come back to us.

I'm truly sorry, Paul, but it's between you and God now. But we will never stop praying for you. What God started in your life, he will finish. If he brings you back to us, it will be in his timing.'

He gave me a last hug and then closed the door behind me.

Chapter 27

Enough Pig Swill

The next fifteen years I would describe as more wilderness years. I lived more or less a nomadic kind of existence. Having made that commitment to Christ at Garston Church, I wasn't going to be able to wriggle out of it. God was always there even though many times I walked away.

I did drink again, many times, and almost overnight I would become ill. It seems unlikely that a loving God would allow this to happen but for this individual, only God in his infinite wisdom knew what was best and always if I drank or took drugs, God would very quickly bring me to my knees. I would equally quickly come back to him, my tail between my legs as a disobedient puppy would come back to its master.

Throughout all this, God was slowly but surely making me strong. At times in prayer I'd ask Him questions like, 'Why, Lord, don't you just snap your fingers and put it all right? You could do it now – this very moment – if you wanted.'

But no, God was showing me time and time again that the free will he'd given me, given all of us, was for a purpose. We would always be faced with choices. That applied very much with his relationship with me. He told me quite clearly, 'Your will or mine, Paul.'

I'm faced every day with the freedom to make that choice. Each time I chose my way, the inevitable would happen – I'd get drunk. How many times God picked me up from the gutter in those days, I couldn't really say. I'd lost count. I'm quite sure that many people in this time put me in the 'no hoper' category, even Christians whom I met along the way.

I'd like to share some of the amazing things that God was showing me through these times.

God's love towards life's so-called hopeless cases – he pours out his grace so abundantly in this group of people that even as I write I'm filled with awe at what he's done in my life personally. The fact that I'm alive physically is a miracle in itself!

During the time of leaving Watford and the Garston Church, so many miracles have happened for me that it would fill another manuscript.

During one of my spells back in gaol, I found myself on 'A' wing of Brixton prison. I was in a pretty sorry state both physically and even more so spiritually. At this time the prison system throughout the country was at bursting point, it was so overcrowded. And to make things even worse, there was a prison officer's National Strike. Normally a petty criminal like me would have been housed in a cell block of a much lower category than 'A' wing which held many armed robbers, murderers even. Prisoners were just being shoved in a cell that happened to have a spare bed.

On this occasion, I was given a bed in a cell with

a drug smuggler and a murderer. On entering the cell, we three inmates exchanged names. For the time being nothing else was said. It was suffocatingly cramped in that cell which originally had been built to accommodate one man. And to make things worse, the murderer (who I'll call Fred) was pacing up and down the small space between my bed and the bunks that he and Terry, the drug smuggler, shared. When I could, I got a glimpse of his face. He looked a very disturbed individual as he paced back and forth in that cell. He was also naked apart from a pair of boxer shorts. Already I felt quite ill from alcohol but this man was really putting the wind up me. Silently, I cried out to Jesus to protect me. There was a table in the cell. One of the legs was supported underneath with a book to stop it wobbling. It was a Bible. My eyes kept going from the murderer to the Bible. How much I wanted that Bible right now. Even just to hold it would comfort me; I knew that. Suddenly, I became aware that Fred had stopped by my bed where I was under the covers with all my clothes on. I was shaking from withdrawal but more so with fear.

Fred spoke. He wasn't looking at me. He just stared straight ahead and said, 'You keep looking at that Bible, don't you, pal? You a Christian or what?' Now he looked at me, waiting for my reply. If I denied my belief in Jesus, what would happen? If I said to this bloke, 'Yes, I believe and I'm a Christian,' what might his reaction be? Even in this situation, God had given me a choice. Deny Jesus or be faithful and honour His Name, even before a murderer. God had never failed me before. I wouldn't deny Jesus. So I went for it.

'Yeah, err, I was looking at the Bible, mate. And,

err, I am a Christian. I've messed up again and here I am, but I know Jesus still loves me.'

There! It was done! Now I waited. He went over to the table, slid the Bible out from beneath the wobbly leg and came back and gave it to me.

'It will be more use to you, then, won't it, than to that lump of wood?' Then he carried on walking up and down. Turning to Psalm 23, I read the comforting words it contained:

> 'The Lord is my shepherd, I shall not be in want.
> He makes me lie down in green pastures,
> He leads me beside quiet waters,
> He restores my soul.
> He guides me in paths of righteousness for His name's sake.
> Even though I walk through the valley of the shadow of death,
> I will fear no evil,
> For You are with me;
> Your rod and Your staff,
> They comfort me.
> You prepare a table before me
> In the presence of my enemies.
> You anoint my head with oil;
> My cup overflows.
> Surely, goodness and mercy will follow me
> all the days of my life,
> And I will dwell in the house of the Lord
> for ever.

The murderer was standing by my bed again. He spoke. 'I've got a lot of time for that Jesus bloke. Don't know that you could call me a Christian

244

though. Too far gone, I am. But Jesus – he had a really hard time didn't he? If I'm found guilty of my crime, I'll get life, because I deserve it. They killed that poor bloke, even though he was completely innocent. Yeah, I've got a lot of time for Jesus. You read your Bible, mate, if it helps. Don't mind me. I'm past all help.'

'Thanks, Fred' was all I could say. That man had summed up the reason for Christ's death in that simple statement and he probably didn't even realise it.

I saw the cross and what it really meant that night. Jesus died between two murderers. Two no-hopers, and yet even in his last breath, one of them recognised Jesus' innocence, just like this murderer in the cell, and because he recognised his own sin at the point of death, Jesus was able to forgive him and assure him of a place in eternity with him. So for Fred, I just pray that he too, wherever he is today, might find the same forgiveness as the murderer at Calvary.

Another time, I was living rough and walking past a pub when I was set upon by two drug-crazed individuals. I fought back, but one of them produced a knife. Turning to run, he pushed the knife in my back. I was rushed to hospital. The knife had penetrated my lung and nearly killed me. Again, I cried out to God to let me live. He did – proof again that although I was not right with him at the time, he is the God of Grace and Mercy he claims to be.

I could go on and on; there are so many experiences that I know to be miracles.

Often I would make plans to return to Watford and Garston Church. Spiritually, it was where God was taking me, of that I was sure, but not yet. Somehow, it wasn't the right time. God was very much still dealing with me.

I longed for a partner, but I wanted someone to share my love of God with. I began to pray for a Christian partner. I settled in Oxford for a while and joined a Pentecostal Church there. I lived in a hostel. My accommodation was basic. I was given a small room to sleep in and meals were provided in a canteen. Some of the staff were Christians and a small group of residents met once a week for prayer. We prayed for our individual needs. My prayer request every week was for a wife. I was lonely. Not only that, God was showing me that I was a person who could love. Sometimes I would pass a vagrant in a street or on a park bench drinking, and my heart would go out to them because I knew that God loved those vagrants as much as me or anyone else.

My periods of sobriety were becoming longer and longer. I was no longer waking up in hospital or prison. I moved again, this time to Swindon. Why Swindon? God only knew that, but that's where I went. Finding a place to sleep in a Salvation Army hostel, I bumped into a man from Watford who I knew. He, like me, had been plagued by alcoholism all his life. Bernie had given his heart to the Lord as well. He asked me to accompany him to the church he was fellowshipping with, an Elim church. We went together that first Sunday. There was a call after to come forward for prayer. I recommitted my life to Jesus that Sunday. And I also asked people to pray that God would give me a wife. Humanly, it would seem an impossibility that anyone would want a person like me with such a shady past.

Again, God would show me that nothing was impossible for Him.

After one of the Sunday Services, an Irish lady approached me and said that God wanted me to attend the midweek prayer meeting. She didn't know specifically why but asked if I would come. Agreeing to come, it seemed a good thing to get involved in fellowship of any kind.

The next day, Monday, I went to the prayer meeting. There were just a few others present. In fact, apart from the ministry team, there were just two of us – myself and a female. The moment I set eyes on this woman, something both spiritual and physical happened. Not only was I attracted physically to her, but much more. Then I knew why I was at this prayer meeting. This woman, her name was Deborah, was the wife I'd been praying for.

After the meeting we just said 'Hello,' no more than that. I went back to the hostel and prayed for God to confirm what I'd felt.

Doing some odd jobs around the church one day, I bumped into Deborah again. Once more, I was to be amazed by God. Deborah was a recovered alcoholic. She hadn't touched a drink for three years. She had been, like me, hopelessly addicted to alcohol and walked an almost identical lifestyle to me. I was sure this was God's confirmation. She invited me to visit her at her parents' home soon after. Her parents, Gordon and Jean Stone, gave me a fairly cool reception. It was obvious they didn't approve and I was saddened by this. However, if this was God's chosen partner for me, nothing would stand in the way. Several more visits followed the same cool reception. They didn't want me around; that was obvious. Deborah began to visit me at the Salvation Army Hostel. It did seem a hopeless situation: here was a penniless, unemployed ex-drunk believing that this was my wife, although I was yet to tell her this.

I went to call for her one day at her family home and was met at the door by her father. He wouldn't let me in. He told me to wait outside. A while after, Deborah came out looking a bit bewildered. She said, 'Dad's just thrown me out. He gave me a choice: either not to see you again, or if I continued to see you, to leave the family home.' She indicated her bag of belongings as to the choice she had made.

It was then I told her that was in love with her and wanted her to be my wife. She said I must be mad, that we hardly knew each other. But she wondered what had made her walk out of her home like this. She said, 'Maybe I like you a lot, but hadn't you better slow down a bit?'

Meanwhile, she was homeless and in many ways it was my fault. Deborah moved into the Ladies' Section of the Salvation Army Hostel.

After I'd shared with Deborah that I believed God had put us together, even though the circumstances seemed a bit much, we began to pray together about it every day. We prayed daily for six months. In that six months I twice got drunk out of frustration and impatience for God to get a move on. Deborah stood by me. Eventually, God spoke to both of us. We knew it was right: we loved each other. I bought an engagement ring and gave it to Debbie over a cup of coffee.

Now we had to pray for a breakthrough at her family home. It came quicker than expected. Gordon opened the door for Deborah to move back in and I was again visiting her. One day, out of respect for Deborah's father and mother, I pleaded with him to give his blessing for us to marry. At the same time, I told him about my background. He listened without interrupting. I wanted to make him understand that I loved Deborah, and whether he would give us his blessing or not, we would still marry – but I would dearly love his consent. He gave us his blessing.

We contacted a Christian ministry that we both had passed through in our drinking days and offered our services there in exchange for somewhere to live so that we could get married. Again, God had gone ahead. They agreed to give us accommodation in return for duties at their day centre for homeless addicts. Deborah and I had both discovered that we had in the past used their rehabilitation programme at separate times. It was based in High Wycombe.

We were going to settle for a civil wedding in High Wycombe Registry Office. We couldn't afford much else. We rang Deborah's father at Swindon and told him what date we would be married and would he please come. He agreed. Deborah wanted so much to have a church wedding. She told me how much she wanted to wear a beautiful wedding dress. She wanted it to really be a marriage made in Heaven. I felt so inadequate; I had no money and didn't even have a suit. We began to wonder if we had made a mistake. We went into earnest prayer together and separately for God to provide another miracle.

The day of the Registry Office ceremony drew near. About a week before, we were invited to a birthday party. Someone pointed out to me that one of the guests was the pastor of a local Elim church. I introduced myself to him and we chatted.

'Oh, I understand you're about to marry then, are you Paul?' the pastor asked.

'Yes, I'm going to marry Deborah,' I replied a little uncertainly.

'Which church have you chosen?' He looked at me.

'Well, we thought a civil thing, really. I've been married before – divorced now. Didn't think it right to marry in church again. Besides we don't have any money for a wedding dress and all the other things.'

'Well, let me ask you first of all – are you a Christian?'

I answered that yes, I was, and that I was born again.

'So, Paul, you are a new creation. Your past is dead. You didn't know Christ as your personal friend and Saviour when you married before, did you?' he asked.

'No, I didn't,' I replied.

'I'll marry you at my church – how does that sound?' he said.

I didn't hesitate with my answer. 'Yes, I'd really like that!'

'Let me have a date for the big day then. God bless you, Paul.'

On the 8th of May, 1993, Deborah and I were married. Deborah wore a white wedding dress which she chose and that was paid for by her father – the cost almost a thousand pounds. There were six bridesmaids. My wife had her marriage made in Heaven. The banqueting hall of a country pub was hired and we had a full buffet and entertainment laid on for 60 guests. The total cost for the day came to over £6,000. The whole bill was picked up by Gordon Stone, now my father-in-law. The same man not long before that day wouldn't have me in his house. Today he treats me like a son. Another miracle which I continually thank God for.

Deborah and I now live back in Watford. Gordon Hickson, who along with the nurse called Rachel, were the instruments used eventually to bring me to Jesus. Gordon is today Pastor of Garston Fellowship (now Watford Community Church). After many years in the wilderness, God had brought me back to the people who, by the world's standards, should have turned their backs on me a long time ago.

For fifteen years or more, members of that family at Garston continued faithfully to pray for me, believing that God would have his way in my life. I'm living proof that God is faithful, even when we are not.

Today, my wife and I do not drink alcohol. I'm hesitant even to take prescribed drugs. I have no desire to get drunk or stoned. God has freed me completely from my addiction to alcohol.

We all in many ways were no-hopers, some not as obvious as others. I am convinced that Jesus Christ can change lives at the twinkling of an eye, or slowly but surely. God sees the heart and just a mustard seed of faith is enough for him to work with.

I've also discovered that it is not wimpish to be a Christian – it's a battle. But now, when the going gets tough, I remember that the battle is really God's, not ours.

I'm human as well as Christian, with feet made of

clay. I'll always make mistakes. Today I still don't have a lot of money, but Debbie and I have never gone hungry. We don't have a car. We don't own our home. But we have each other by God's grace. Today, we are not in prison. Today we are not insane with a wet brain. Today we are alive. Today I'm happy. Today this so-called 'no hoper' of the past has all hope.

When I last saw Alan Vincent, I reminded him of his last words when he saw me off at the door all those years ago. 'Alan,' I said, 'I've come home, and believe me, I didn't leave a lot of pig swill behind.'

We had a good laugh at that. But we both really knew what I meant. God had brought me full circle, from pig swill to his banqueting table.